About the author:
Dr. Moira Chan-Yeung is Professor Emeritus of Medicine at the University of British Columbia and Honorary Clinical Professor of Medicine at the University of Hong Kong. This book is her sixth scholarly work on history after her retirement.

Other history books by the author:
Fung, Y.W., Chan-Yeung, M. *To Serve and to Lead- A History of Diocesan Boys' School*. Hong Kong: Hong Kong University Press, 2009.
Chan-Yeung, M. *The Practical Prophet: Bishop Ronald O Hall and His Hong Kong Legacy*. Hong Kong: Hong Kong University Press, 2015.
Chan-Yeung, M. *Lam Woo: Master Builder, Revolutionary and Philanthropist. Hong Kong*: Hong Kong: The Chinese University Press, 2017
陳慕華著，馮以浤譯．林護．孫中山背後的香港建築商．香港中文大學出版社，2017
Chan-Yeung, M. *A Medical History of Hong Kong 1842-1941*. Hong Kong: The Chinese University Press, 2018.
Chan-Yeung M. *A Medical History of Hong Kong 1942-2015*. Hong Kong: The Chinese University Press, in press.

Chen Qiyuan:

Pioneer of Modern Chinese Industry, Entrepreneur, Philanthropist

Moira M. W. Chan-Yeung

Chen Qiyuan
Pioneer of Modern Chinese Industry, Entrepreneur, Philanthropist
   By Moira M. W. Chan-Yeung

All rights reserved. No part of this publication may be reproduced or transmitted without permission in writing from the author.

ISBN-13: 978-1722424527

Contents

Preface	vii
Acknowledgments	xiii
Family of Chen Qiyuan	xv
Introduction	1
Chapter 1: Silk Industry Development in China	9
Chapter 2: Life in Jiancun, Xiqiao (1836–1854)	33
Chapter 3: Years in Annam (1854–1872)	59
Chapter 4: Jichanglong—The First Chinese Silk Filature in South China	95
Chapter 5: The 1881 Silk Weavers' Riot and the Macau Interlude (1882–1885)	119
Chapter 6: Achievements in Later Years (1885–1904)	143
Chapter 7: Contributions of Chen Qiyuan and Their Impact	177
Epilogue	193
Notes	197
Appendix 1: Life Events of Chen Qiyuan	225
Appendix 2: Bibliography	229
Appendix 3: Selected Pictures	241
Glossary of English and Chinese Names and Index	247

Preface

Chen Qiyuan had been recognized as a national entrepreneur and a great patriot of his mother country, the People's Republic of China. A memorial hall had been dedicated to honor him in his native village Jiancun, Xiqiao, Nanhai, Guangdong, a place where he was born and lived, excluding a long sojourn of about 18 years in Annam (present-day Vietnam). It was in Annam where he became a wealthy businessman and acquired the knowledge and technology of the modern silk industry.

    I am one of Qiyuan's numerous descendants, the second granddaughter of Qiyuan's ninth and youngest son, Chen Ruzhi. When I turned two years old, Japanese occupation of Hong Kong began and we stayed in our grandfather's house on Bonham Road in Hong Kong. Our kindergarten and part of primary education fell on my grandfather, who patiently taught my siblings and me the use of the brush to write Chinese, how to do simple arithmetic, and told us stories about his father, Chen Qiyuan, especially of his remarkable and superhuman eyesight. According to my grandfather, Qiyuan was able to read signboards located in Tismshatsui across the harbor from Hong Kong, had carved a poem on small pieces of ivory of the size of sesame seeds, and had written in beautiful calligraphy a Chinese dictionary of almost 50,000 words on the front and back of a fan. Yet, when I looked around at my relatives and my own siblings, everyone wore corrective eyeglasses for shortsightedness. I ceased to pay attention to the other stories about him, especially those related to the shipwreck on his way to Annam.

After the war, we moved from our grandfather's house. My studies and my career took me away from Hong Kong for over 30 years. When I returned to Hong Kong in 1998, I heard that my great grandfather had been honored with a memorial hall named after him, and later still, he was named one of the 56 sages of South Guangdong (南粵先賢).

It was many years after my retirement that I decided to trace my roots and visit my famous ancestor's memorial hall in Nanhai. I was attracted to this studious, serious-looking, innovative, altruistic individual, who, despite all odds, realized his dream of making his impoverished native village and the Pearl River Delta into a relatively prosperous region by inventing a machine for silk reeling. This technology, though not world-shattering by any means, not only increased the efficiency of silk reeling, but also improved the quality of the silk for export. Qiyuan did not patent his invention but gladly taught people how to make the machine and how to run the business. He gave the blueprints of his machine to anyone who asked for them.

Because Qiyuan shared his innovation widely and freely, silk filatures mushroomed in the Pearl River Delta Region in the late nineteenth century and the early twentieth century for almost five decades. Silk became the largest export item, bringing in wealth and prosperity for the people in the Pearl River Delta Region. The growth of the silk industry acted as a catalyst for the development of other industries such as machinery, energy, finance, and trade. He also pioneered innovations in management, including the introduction of a female labor force to work alongside men. Such a brave experiment in China at that time resulted in immense social changes.

Largely a self-educated man, Qiyuan authored several books, including one on sericulture and another on mathematics. One can even find his name in *Cihai*, a large-scale, comprehensive Chinese dictionary and encyclopedia.

By the time I was ready to research into the life of my great grandfather, I found that there had already been three books written in Chinese about him: 1) *Chen Qiyuan* by Wu Jianxin, published by Guangdong People Publishing House in 2012, (吳建新,"陳啟沅", 廣州:廣東人民出版社); 2) *The Turbulent History of the Silk Industry: Chen Qiyuan: a Pioneer in Modern Industry in China* by Chen Zuohai, published by South China Technology University Press, 2016, (陳作海, 繅絲風雲錄: 記中國近代民族工業先驅陳啟沅, 廣州:華南理工大学出版社); 3) "A Critical Review of the Life of Chen Qiyuan by Xu Feng, currently in press (許鋒, 陳啟沅評傳").

The first book by Wu Jianxin consists of all the essential and confirmed records of Chen Qiyuan's life according to the Annals of Nanhai County. Chen Zouhai, author of the second book, is the youngest surviving grandson of Chen Qiyuan. Zouhai spent a great deal of time researching into his grandfather's life in Qiyuan's native village in Nanhai. His book includes many details about the childhood of Chen Qiyuan and accounts of his years in Annam, mainly taken from family stories handed down from generation to generation. The third book by Xu Feng is more academic, with references both from primary and secondary sources, adding information of Chen Qiyuan's life in Macau between 1881 and 1883, which is lacking in the above two books. As these three books were all written in Chinese, and Chen Qiyuan had many descendants living in different parts of the world, who may not be proficient in Chinese and may not have knowledge of their illustrious ancestor, I felt that a book about him in English would be useful and timely. Chen Qiyuan, epitomized by his altruism, generosity, devotion to his countrymen, and steadfastness of purpose despite obstacles and failure, was a shining example for all to emulate, not only his descendants.

Instead of translating any one of the above three books into English, I have decided to write my own story, incorporating events recorded in the three books and those from my own research, as my tribute to this selfless, patriotic man, who, in addition to donating his invention to improve the livelihood of his native village, used his wealth in many philanthropic activities, such as creating schools, establishing charitable medical clinics, and arranging burials for those whose family could not afford to do so. He used his own ingenuity and technical skills to improve water drainage in his village and also settled a dispute of mining rights between three parties in an antimony mine in Shaoquan, Guangdong, that no one had been able to do before, by using his knowledge of survey.

This book has seven chapters. The first chapter is a brief history of development of the silk industry in China, the second describes Chen Qiyuan's childhood in Jiancun, and the third contains information about his years in Annam and how he learned the technology necessary to build the silk reeling machines. The fourth chapter recounts how he built the filature, Jichanglong, in his native Jiancun. The fifth chapter is the story of the silk weavers' riot and how Jichanglong was forced to close by the government and move to Macau, and how Qiyuan and his son invented a "bicycle silk-reeling machine" that could produce high quality silk for home use. The sixth chapter summarizes his achievements in later years, and the final chapter discusses Chen Qiyuan's contributions and their impact on the silk industry, as well as socio-economic changes to the Pearl River Delta Region.

The materials in this book came from the three books as mentioned above, and from information in the County Annals of Nanhai, and from books and theses on the silk industry in China as detailed in Appendix 2.

Moira M.W. Chan-Yeung
May 2018

Acknowledgements

I am indebted to many relatives, who assisted in the preparation of this book: Chen Zuohai, my uncle, who has written a book about Chen Qiyuan and sent me materials; Chen Shuhua, my cousin, for newsprints and other materials on Chen Qiyuan; Ronnie Chan, my brother, for providing a set of pictures of the Chen Qiyuan Memorial Hall and a number of books from China; May Kaan, my sister, for her set of pictures of the Chen Qiyuan Memorial Hall expertly taken; Grace Wong, my niece, for the photographs of the old Xiguan residence of Chen Qiyuan and Chen Puxian; Keith Poon, my cousin, for materials on Cholon; David Yeung, my husband, for his photographs and Mark Yeung, my son, for designing the front and back cover and other technical help. May and Grace also kindly read over the manuscript for mistakes. This book, indeed, is a combined effort of the Chan family.

I am most thankful to Professor David Faure and Professor He Xi of the Chinese University of Hong Kong for their kindness in sending me copies of three documents of ancestral records of Chen Ruzhi. These documents had been presented to Professor Faure of the Department of History by my late cousin Dr. Man Si-wai. I am beholden to the curator of Chen Qiyuan Memorial Hall for permission to use our photographs of the Memorial Hall and its exhibits in the book, Stanley Young for his assistance with the maps, Sarah Weinstein for editing and

Lyle Weinstein for his assistance in all aspects of publication. My gratitude also goes to Dr. Kenneth Suen for his most insightful comments and for his careful editing of the manuscript; and Mr. Fung Yee Wang, who had gone ever the manuscript with great care, corrected my English translation of Chinese terms, and gave his critical comments.

Family of Chen Qiyuan

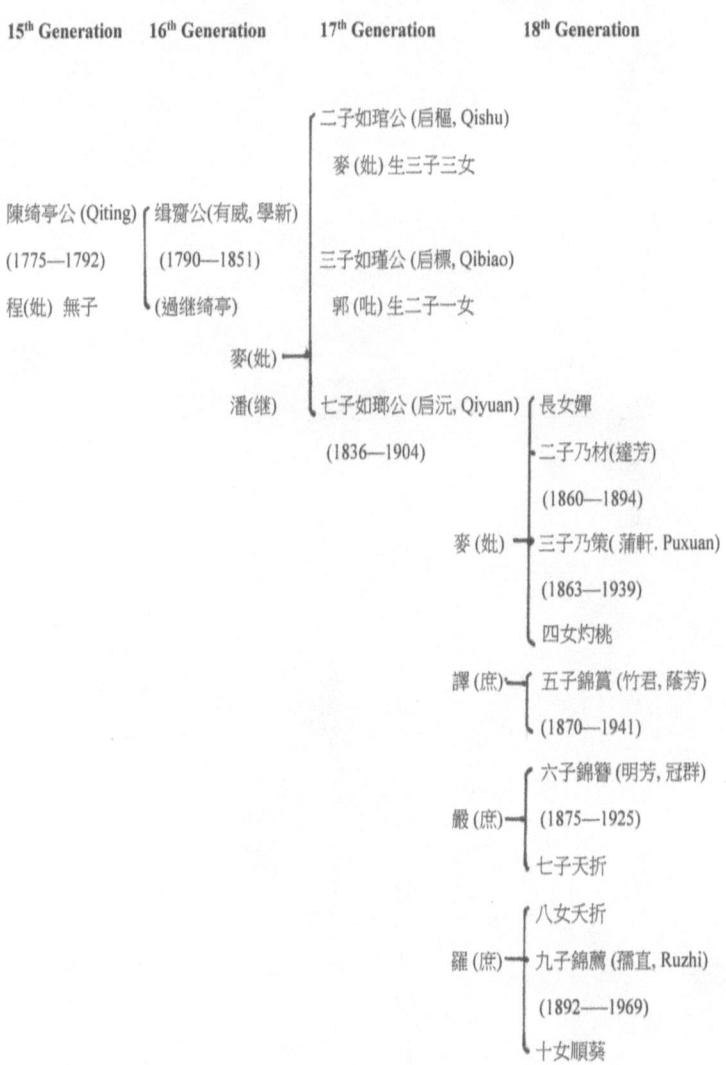

Introduction

Xiqiao (西樵), in the southwest of Guangzhou (廣州), is dominated by a mountain, Xiqiao Mountain (西樵山), which is the site of an old extinguished volcano. Rice fields, fish ponds, and mulberry trees spread from the foot of Xiqiao Mountain and cover miles of its surroundings. Because of its beauty, serenity, and picturesque landscape of lakes, waterfalls, and springs amidst caves and peaks, Xiqiao Mountain has attracted visitors from all over the country, and in the old days literati like writers and poets.

Situated at the foot of Xiqiao Mountain is Jiancun (簡村), one of several villages in the area. A stream runs lazily through the middle of the village. Long, narrow boats, as though tailor-made for the meandering stream, are moored on either side, waiting patiently for their owners or customers. There is hardly any movement on the stream to disturb the serenity of the village. This must be a far cry from the old days when narrow boats busily carried all kinds of materials such as cocoons, mulberry leaves, or reeled silk to the markets, and other raw materials including fuel to various filatures in the area. Where the stream meanders and makes a loop stands an old house, the ancestral home of the Chen family. It was originally built by Chen Qiyuan (陳啟沅) in 1887 as the Chen Qiting Ancestral Hall (陳绮亭公祠). In 1994, the government of the county of Nanhai extensively renovated the whole compound and changed the name of the Ancestral Hall to "Chen Qiyuan Memorial Hall (陳啟沅紀念館)" to honor Chen Qiyuan for his numerous contributions to the region and his selflessness and patriotism.[1]

The compound occupies an area of 1,500 square meters and the buildings 600 square meters. It can be divided into two parts: the first part consists of exhibition rooms of the Memorial Hall, and the second part includes the Mulberry and Silkworm Garden (蠶桑園) and Joy of Farming *si-shu* (樂耕堂).[2]

Chen Qiyuan Memorial Hall (Figure i.1) is a typical *siheyuan* (四合院),[3] which means a courtyard surrounded by four buildings. The buildings, roofs, and some of the doors have ornate decorations (Figure i.2, i.3).

Figure i.1. Main entrance to Chen Qiyuan Memorial Hall in Jiancun, Xiqiao, Nanhai (photo by author)

Figure i.2. Decorative panels separate the exhibition room from the courtyard (photo by Ronnie Chan)

Figure i.3. Ornate roof of Chen Qiyuan Memorial Hall (photo by Ronnie Chan)

Figure i.4. Bust of Chen Qiyuan (photo by author)

When one enters the Ancestral Hall of Chen Qiting, one immediately encounters the bust of Chen Qiyuan in traditional Chinese attire, showing his pointed head, protuberant forehead, a straight and upright nose bridge, a wisp of beard, and a very serious expression (Figure i.4). Below the bust is a plaque where the life and achievements of Chen Qiyuan are inscribed (Figure i.5).

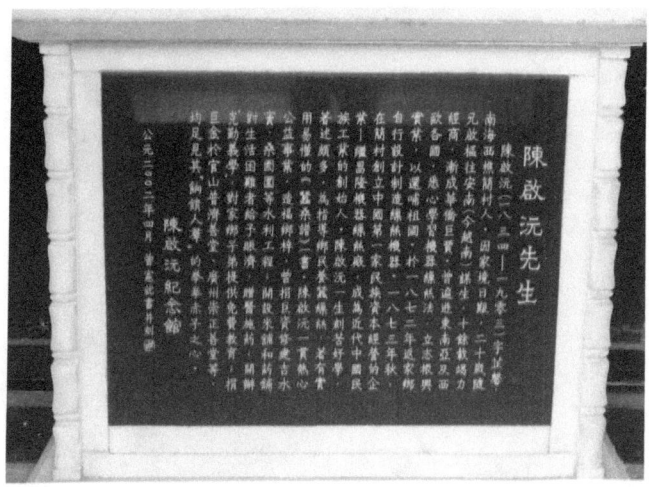

Figure i.5. The plaque beneath the bust of Chen Qiyuan with the story of his lie (photo by May Kaan)

This room leads to a courtyard, surrounded by larger rooms with exhibits on two sides of the quadrangle, displaying pictures, materials, and models telling Chen Qiyuan's life story, and showing the machines that he had invented for silk reeling along with the books that he had written.

The Mulberry and Silkworm Garden (Figure i.6), the second portion of the compound, has a luxurious growth of mulberry trees with a fish pond in the middle. Three tall Guanglangshu (桄榔樹, *Arenga pinnata*, commonly called Sugar Palm Tree) stand proudly next to it (Figure i.7). They were planted by Chen Qiyuan himself in 1887. While Chen and his descendants come and go, these trees withstand the passage of time. The *si-shu*, Joy of Farming, occupies one end of the garden while the silkworm room the other (Figure i.8).

Figure i.6. Entrance to the Silkworm and Mulberry Garden (photo by Ronnie Chan)

Figure i.7. The three Guanglangshu planted by Chen Qiyuan (photo by David Yeung)

Figure i.8. Silkworm room with ornate roof and panels (photo by David Yeung)

Chen Qiyuan lived an extraordinary life. He fully utilized his unusual gift of superior eyesight and intelligence to struggle against all odds and brought prosperity to his native village and the Pearl River Delta Region. He invented the first Chinese silk reeling machine and started the industrialization of the souther China. His selfless devotion to diffusing his knowledge and invention stimulated the development and economy in the region during and after his lifetime. His enormous contributions and his numerous philanthropic activities earned the honor bestowed upon him almost one hundred years after his death.

Chapter 1: Silk Industry Development in China

To comprehend the significance of Chen Qiyuan's work in the development of the silk industry in China and its impact, it is necessary to have some understanding of the Chinese silk industry before and after his time and how his work had contributed to the industry as a whole.

How Silk Is Made

Silk is an animal fiber produced by the caterpillars of the domesticated silk moth, *Bombyx mori*. The term "silkworm" refers to the caterpillar (larva) of the moth. Silk is the product of a series of stages, starting from the cultivation of mulberry trees whose leaves are the primary food source for the larvae. During the larval or caterpillar phase, the silkworm secretes a liquid protein that hardens into a filament upon exposure to air. A second protein, sericin, is then secreted to bind the filament, which forms a thick sheath, known as a cocoon, surrounding the worm. Under natural conditions through metamorphosis, a moth eventually emerges through the cocoon, and disrupts the continuity of the silk filament. In sericulture (silk farming), the moth in the chrysalis stage inside the cocoon is killed by steam or hot air to prevent hatching. The cocoons are then dried, sorted according to quality, and stored (Figure 1.1). Appropriate cocoon-drying techniques and reeling operations are vital to the manufacturing of good quality silk.

Figure 1.1. Cocoons and moths displayed in Chen Qiyuan Memorial Hall (photo by David Yeung)

The length of a single unbroken silk filament of a cocoon produced by the silkworm measures from 500 to 1,000 meters in length. Before the silk filament can be used, carefully controlled heated water is used to soften the sericin, the gummy material secreted by the silkworms. The degumming process facilitates the unwinding of filaments from cocoons without breakage. During the silk reeling process, several filaments are combined with a slight twist into one strand, as single filaments are too thin for commercial use.[1]

History of the Silk Industry in China

Silk is a highly priced commodity even though its trade volume is less than 1% of the market for natural textile fibers. Silk is acclaimed as the "Queen of Textiles" due to its exclusive beauty. Silk production in China can be dated back more than 3,000 years as far as the Shang Dynasty (1600 BCE–1046 BCE). It started in the Yellow River Basin where mulberry and silkworm cultivation was first found. In the Western Han Dynasty (206 BCE–8 CE), limited quantities of silk goods were transported overland along the Silk Route via the Hexi Corridor (河西走廊) and the Tarim Basin (塔里木盆地) through Central Asia to the Roman Empire. In North China, cotton growing soon overtook silk production, because cotton is good for keeping the wearer warm in winter and somewhat cool in warmer climates. In South China, sericulture was not popular until refugees from North China brought with them the knowledge of the silk industry when North China was invaded by successive waves of nomads between the fourth and the sixth centuries. During the Northern Song Dynasty (960 CE–1127 CE), the center of silk production moved southwards to the present-day Jiangsu-Zhejiang (江蘇-浙江) and to Guangdong (廣東). Even on the Yangtze Delta, sericulture gave way to cotton cultivation, because cotton suited the needs of the people. Sericulture, however, persisted in certain regions such as Huzhou.[2] Over the centuries, China has developed several centers for sericulture, but the two major ones are in Yangtze River Delta (Jiangnan, 江南) Region and the Pearl River Delta (Figure 1.2).

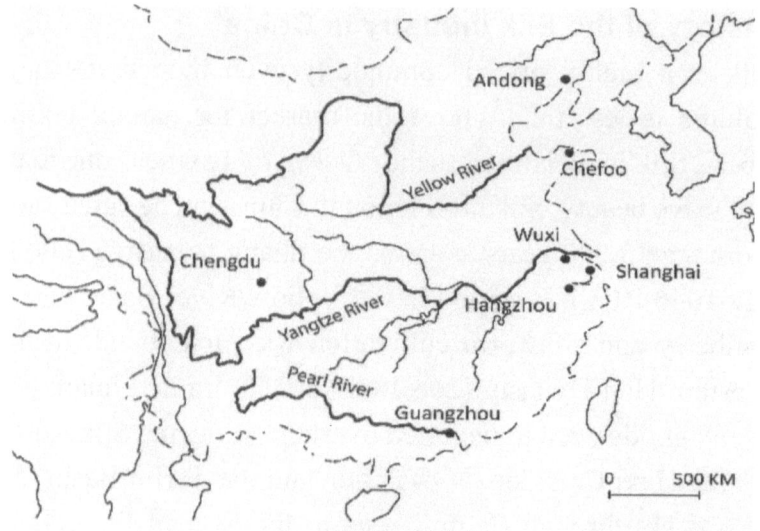

Figure 1.2. Major silk producing centers in China (modified from R. Eng, Major sik producing areas in early Republican China, University of California, Center for Chinese studies, 1986, x, map 1)

Commercialization of sericulture began in the Yuan Dynasty (1271–1368 CE) and increased in the Ming Dynasty (1368–1644 CE). In the mid-sixteenth century, Chinese-Spanish trade flourished through the Philippines. Silk goods and silk fabric from China were sold to the Americas by the Spanish. The Chinese were paid with silver from the Americas. Thus, the silk trade became important to the Chinese economy. Even then the amount of raw silk exported was less than 4,000 *piculs* (擔) (1 *picul* = 60.5 kilograms) per year. The reduction in silver supply in the seventeenth century led to the decline of silk exports and also to severe deflationary pressure on the Chinese economy, which contributed to the fall of the Ming Dynasty.

At the beginning of the nineteenth century, raw silk exports increased and reached 10,000 *piculs* (Figure 1.3). Even then mulberry production, silkworm raising, and silk reeling were still carried out in the rural areas by peasants. Urban weaving shops remained small in size and were limited to about 20 workers. Chinese silk goods were principally for the domestic market. It was not until after the opening of the five treaty ports that Chinese silk export began to surge. The unequal treaties of 1842 facilitated not only the import of foreign manufactured goods but also the export of raw materials from China.[3]

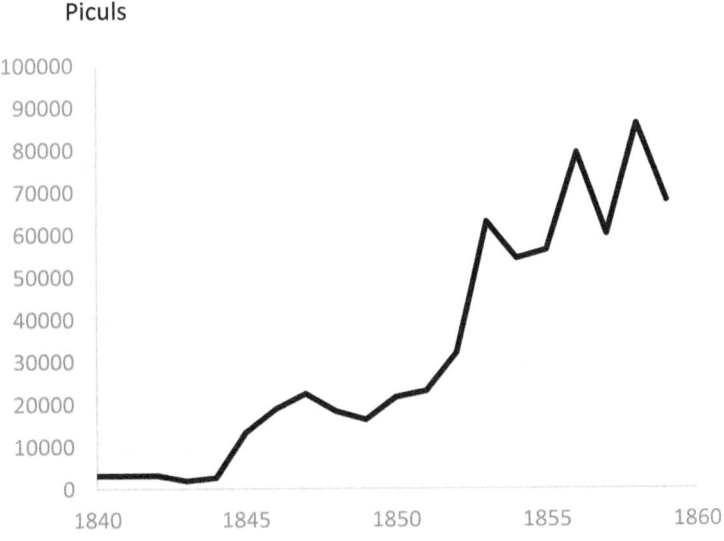

Figure 1.3. Raw silk exports from China, 1840–1859, in bales (1 bale=60.5 kg.) (Source: Eng, Major silk producing areas in early Republican China, 26)

From 1854 to 1872, silk export from China greatly expanded for several reasons. First, foreign demand escalated. In 1854, the pébrine silkworm disease[4] devastated sericulture in Europe, leading to a dramatic increase in demand of raw silk from China. At that time, France had become the world's leading producer and exporter of silk goods. Even though its sericulture suffered, French silk weaving sector continued to prosper, and France had to import about two-thirds of raw silk for its own needs. The demand from the United States also grew as it became an industrial power. In 1864, in order to raise revenue for the Civil War in the United States, the tariff on imported silk goods was raised to 60%, while raw silk was admitted free of duty. In the United States, sericulture was almost nonexistent because it was labor-intensive and labor cost was high; therefore, the United States imported all of its raw silk. Between 1874 and 1890, the demand for raw silk from the United States increased by 16 times.[5] This swell in French and American demand for raw silk led to an upsurge in Chinese raw silk export and changes in the mode of production.

Second, the expansion of Chinese exports to other parts of the world was greatly facilitated by the revolution in transport and communication between east and west in the second half of the nineteenth century. In 1867, the opening of direct services to China by the Pacific Mail Steamship Company made possible the direct import of raw silk into the United States from the Far East. In 1871, the completion of the Far Eastern section of the submarine telegraph cable, linking Shanghai, Hong Kong, and Singapore, put Shanghai into direct telegraphic communication with London, which was the center for raw silk distribution in 1880. Third, the depreciation of silver relative to gold in the second half of the nineteenth century to the early part of the twentieth century also favored the expansion of Chinese exports in general.[6]

Before the 1870s, silk production in China was largely a peasant activity primarily carried out by women in the household using primitive machinery. Because the hand-reels for silk reeling did not require much capital investment, the women worked in their own homes, used their own tools, and produced their own reeled silk. They were involved in mulberry cultivation, leaf picking, silkworm raising, cocoon collecting and silk reeling. These activities proceeded one after another without interruption throughout the year.[7] The final product, hand-reeled silk, was either purchased by foreign merchants at Guangzhou for the Western weaving industries or it was used by local rural weavers for weaving silk goods for both the domestic and foreign markets.

However, the demand for raw silk by Western countries was not only for quantity but also quality, which could not be met by hand-reeled silk. China, which had been producing and exporting the largest quantity of raw silk so far, was beginning to lose its premier position in the world market because of the poor quality of hand-reeled silk. Better quality raw silk could only be provided by silk reeled in the filatures using more advanced technology. Chen Qiyuan realized the importance of filature in the development of China's silk industry.

Filature Development

The development of filatures was faster along the Pearl River Delta than those along the Yangtze River Delta. To minimize the cost of transportation of cocoons, filatures were usually built near the areas where sericulture was abundant. In the Pearl River Delta Region, filatures were built in the rural areas in close proximity to sericulture, and the silk produced was exported through Guangzhou (formerly Canton). On the Yangtze River Delta, all filature silk was exported through Shanghai. In this region, some filatures were established in rural areas where cocoons were produced, but a number of filatures were also built in Shanghai, some distance from the cocoon-producing areas.

Chen Qiyuan founded the first filature, Jichanglong, in 1874, in the village of Jiancun (located in Xiqiao Town within the district of Nanhai) and played a crucial role in the rapid development of filatures in the Pearl River Delta Region. Because of lack of infrastructure in China for reproducing the steam-powered Western silk reeling machines that he had learned in depth in Annam, Qiyuan designed his own machine based on the knowledge he acquired and what was available locally in terms of materials and technical help. His enthusiastic sharing of information and his willingness to give assistance to anyone who was interested in establishing a filature led to the establishment of nine other filatures in Nanhai County and a few more in

Shunde (順德) within a few years.⁸ The fierce competition for supply of cocoons between the filatures and the local silk weavers and the danger threatening the latter's livelihood led to the Silk Weavers' Riot in 1881. The riot ended with the closure order of filatures from the local government of Nanhai County.

Although the filatures in Nanhai County were forced to close, filatures located on other parts of the Pearl River Delta were not affected. In Shunde County, filatures proliferated and the County became the regional center for production and export for filature-reeled silk and for cocoon distribution because of its excellent location with extensive waterways for transportation of cocoons.⁹

In the late 1880s, Chen Qiyuan and his son designed a "bicycle silk reeling machine" powered by a foot treadle for domestic use, and it included some features which allowed the quality of silk to be high enough for export. By 1894, there were 75 filatures in Guangdong Province (Table 1.1), growing to about 190 in 1913. Some filatures were powered by steam and they coexisted with a variety of other silk-production models, such as filatures with machines powered by foot treadles but with steam-heated hot water such as Jichanglong, and workrooms with only foot-treadle machines. These filatures and workshops were not in Guangzhou, the capital city and the port of Guangdong Province, but scattered in villages and market towns close to or within the cocoon-producing areas.

Although the first modern silk filature, Ewo (怡和) Filature, a foreign enterprise using modern machines, was

17

founded as early as 1863 in Shanghai, the development of filatures on the Yangtze River Delta was slower than in the Pearl River Delta Region. Ewo Filature was closed in 1869 after going into debt every year since its founding. Because of the Chinese government's official monopoly and prohibition of private ownership by Chinese citizens of any industry, there were few Chinese filatures in Shanghai. In 1891, only three filatures existed in Shanghai, growing to 27 in 1896. Expansion of filatures in Shanghai only began to take place in the early 1910s and continued into 1920s when the number of filatures rose to about 100.[10] On the Yangtze River Delta, there were three filatures in 1897, increasing to 124 in 1927.[11]

Table 1.1. No. of Filatures in Nanhai, Shunde, and Guangdong

Year	Nanhai	Shunde	Total in Guangdong
1873	1		1
1874		1	>2
1875			5
1881	10	5	>16
1883	11	9	>20
1894	20	>50	75

Source: Modified from Wong Chor Yee, "Proto-industrialization and the Silk Industry of the Canton Delta, 1662–1934", (PhD Thesis, University of Madison–Wisconsin, 1995), 308, Table 4.22.

The owners of filatures at the Pearl River Delta Region enjoyed financial advantage over their counterparts in Shanghai, as many of them received a steady flow of remittances from family members who had emigrated aboard. The Shanghai owners for the most part did not have this extra benefit. Chen Qiyuan was only one of the many examples of Chinese capitalists with business experience overseas who invested in the silk filatures back home. There were several others returning from other parts of the world. Many merchants who emigrated from Shunde were engaged with trade overseas and millions were remitted home annually.[12] The financial advantage enjoyed by the owners was partly responsible for the rapid early growth of filatures and of filature-reeled silk for export from the Pearl River Delta Region.

Filatures in the Pearl River Delta Region also enjoyed favorable climatic conditions. Because of milder climate, they could operate 300 days or more each year, at an advantage over Shanghai filatures which could only operate 250 days each year. The farmers on the Pearl River Delta could raise silkworms full-time because the silkworms were multi-voltine (capable of brooding up to eight to nine generations each year). Filature owners in this region could spread out their cocoon purchases throughout the year and required less working capital to run the filature successfully in comparison to their Shanghai counterparts. In the Yangtze River Delta Region, silkworms were uni-voltine (one generation each year) or bi-voltine (two generations per year).[13] Filatures on the Pearl River Delta were all situated in the rural area where sericulture was carried out and transportation of cocoons to the filatures hardly cost much. Shanghai filatures had more difficulties in obtaining a supply of cocoons because cocoons had to be transported from some distances away, and these filatures suffered from closures from time to time due to cocoon shortage.

Mulberry Dike–Fish Pond: A Perfect Ecological System

The growth of the silk industry greatly influenced land use in both regions in China. As the global demand for raw silk swelled in the 1850s and 1860s, sericulture and cultivation of mulberry trees proliferated in both regions. Wheat and rice fields were converted into lucrative mulberry fields, which generated five times more profit. During Tongzhi (同治) Period of the Qing Dynasty (1862–1874), sericulture bureaus, where peasants were taught mulberry growing by officials and gentry, were established in many counties in Jiangsu (江蘇) Province, including Wuxi (無錫), an old township at the coastline of the Yangtze River. By the first decade of the twentieth century, three major sericulture regions could be identified in Jiangsu Province: Wuxi-Changzhou (無錫-常州) area, the Suzhou (蘇州) region, and the northern Jiangsu area, which included the cities of Nanjing (南京) and Zhejiang (浙江) and the area north of Yangtze. Within the Zhejiang Province, there were also three major sericultural regions: the Huzhou (湖州) region south of Lake Tai (太湖), the Suzhou-Jiaxing (蘇州-嘉興) region, and the Shaoxing (紹興) region.[14]

On the Pearl River Delta, since the Ming Dynasty, mulberry growing had been combined with fish rearing (mulberry dike–fish pond), in accordance with the "four water, six land" scheme. Under this scheme, the land in four-tenths of a given area was dug out to form a large pond. Dikes were formed using the excavated soil, upon which mulberry trees were planted, with fish raised in the ponds during the summer and sold during the winter. The remaining six-tenths of the land were used for regular crop growing. Sediments from the ponds were used to fertilize the soil and in turn, silkworm litter and dead silkworms were used to feed the fish, creating a perfect ecological system. The co-production of mulberry-tree growing and sericulture together with fish farming was first introduced in the northern part of the Pearl River Delta. Later on, the co-production spread gradually to the middle and southern parts of the Delta. In the 1860s, mulberries were extensively cultivated in the alluvial counties to the south of Guangzhou. In the 1880s, almost all the land in Shunde County and one-quarter of all the land in Nanhai County were covered with mulberry dike-fish ponds. By the 1890s, Dongguan (東莞) County and Sanshui (三水) County also turned agricultural lands into mulberry plantations and silkworm-rearing areas.[15]

Raw Silk Export

After the 1860s, there was a change in the pattern of silk exported. The increasing demand from the West was for raw silk and not silk goods, which were mainly for the local market, and their export over the years remained low compared with that of raw silk (Figure 1.4).

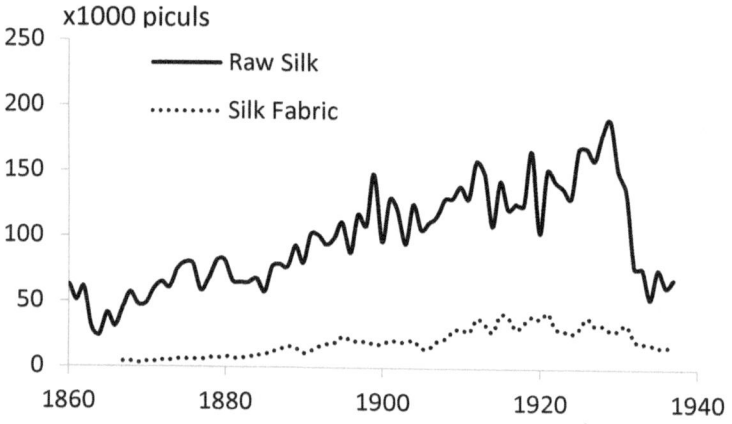

Figure 1.4. Raw silk and silk fabric exports from China, 1859–1937 (Source: Lillian Li, *China's Silk Trade. Traditional Industry in the Modern World, 1842–1937*, Cambridge, Massachusetts and London, 1981, 74–76)

The increase in silk filatures in China led to a rapid rise of filature-reeled raw silk with a concomitant decrease in home-reeled silk for export. By 1900, the export of filature-reeled silk overtook home-reeled silk and continued to rise (Figure 1.5).

In the Pearl River Delta Region, the amount of filature-reeled silk exported rose rapidly and accounted for a greater percentage of total raw silk exported, reaching over 90% in 1900, a level only reached by Shanghai about 10 to 15 years later (Figure 1.6). This could be accounted for by the earlier start in establishment of filatures in the Pearl River Delta Region, spearheaded by Chen Qiyuan, followed rapidly by others.

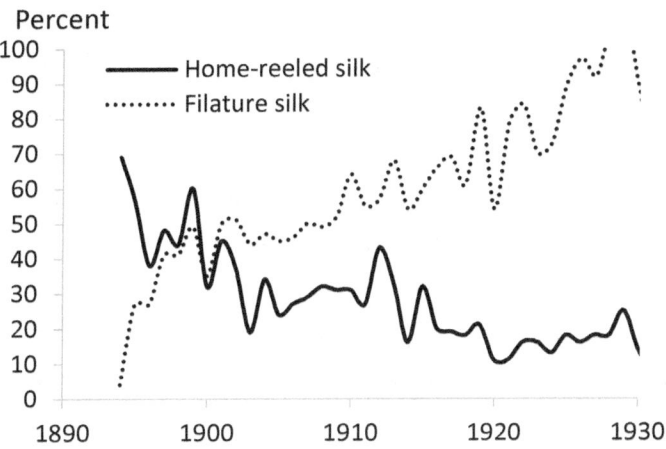

Figure 1.5. Home-reeled and filature-reeled raw silk as % total exported from China, 1894—1932 (Source: Li, *China's Silk Trade. Traditional Industry in the Modern World, 1842–1933*, 80–81)

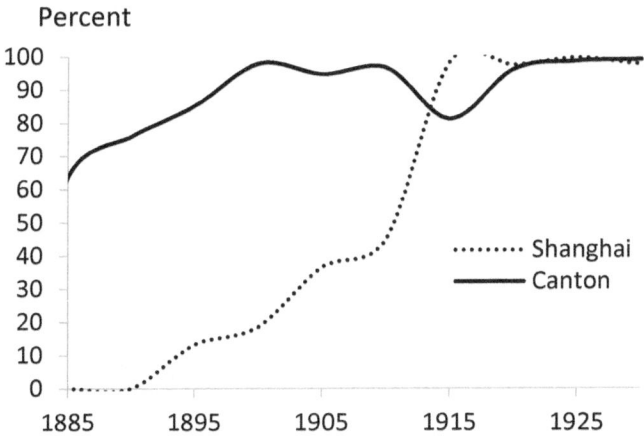

Figure 1.6. Filature-silk as % total silk exported from Shanghai and Guangzhou, 1885–1930 (Source: Li, *Chins's Silk Trade, Traditional Industry in the Modern World, 1842–1933*, 79

China had been the leading country in the world for silk export for centuries. In the late nineteenth and early twentieth centuries, it encountered keen competition from Japan, whose export of filature-reeled raw silk grew rapidly and surpassed China by 1910 (Figure 1.7). Although both countries with their backward feudal systems came under pressure and exploitation of Western countries in the mid-nineteenth century, their response was decidedly different. In Japan, the Meji Restoration in the late 1860s consolidated imperial power, followed by military reform, industrialization, and a change from a feudal society to market economy, resulting in a marked increase in productivity. The Japanese had embraced the reforms wholeheartedly. In China, the Self-Strengthening Movement was mostly restricted to military reforms. The defeat of China by Japan in the Sino-Japanese War in 1894–1895 showed how futile merely reforming the military could be without socioeconomic and political changes. The loss of competitiveness of Chinese raw silk to Japanese was due to many factors, which included the lack of government support and its imposition of high taxes and likins, and the unequal treaties signed with Western nations. Compared with Chinese vessels, Western and Japanese vessels enjoyed a huge advantage in carrying trade because of the minimal tax they needed to pay. Some of the Chinese vessels resorted to flying foreign flags to avoid multiple taxation and extortion by customs officials.[16]

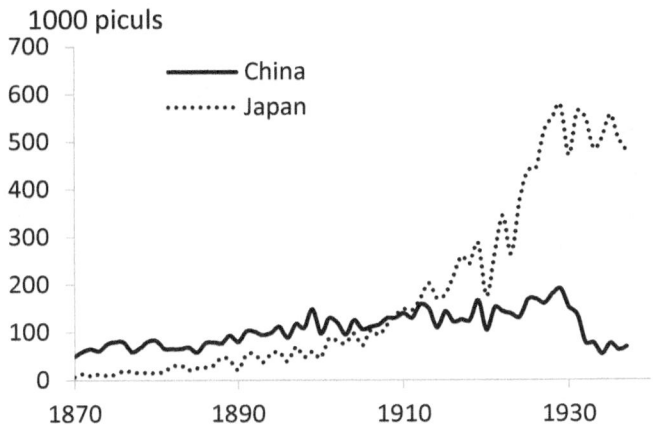

Figure 1.7. Chinese and Japanese raw silk export (in 1000 piculs) 1870–1937 (Source: Li, *China's Silk Trade. Traditional Industry in the Modern World 1842–1937*, 86–88)

Specialization in Different Stages of Silk Production and Its Marketing

Associated with rapid growth of the silk industry, specialization occurred at different levels of the industry in China. In the Yangtze River Delta, it became unusual for mulberry growers to be involved with silkworm rearing. In the Pearl River Delta, probably 50% of mulberry leaves consumed by sericulture farmers were purchased, either by contract between the producer and the buyer or from retailers at the leaf market.[17] In market towns on the Pearl River Delta, there were usually two to three mulberry leaf markets that belonged to lineages or villages. The market operators collected a small commission (2% from sellers and 6% from buyers) for providing the facilities and the weighing services.

Most silkworm raisers were non-growers of mulberry leaves and they purchased silkworm eggs instead of producing their own. In Zhejiang Province, Shaoxing (紹興) and Yuhang (餘杭) were two leading counties specializing in the production of silkworm eggs, and they supplied the whole province and other parts of the Yangtze River Delta Region. In Guangdong Province, the production of silkworm eggs was also undertaken separately, and they were sold at special egg markets that also belonged to lineages or villages.

Cocoon markets sprang up in different parts of Xiqiao in the 1870s.[18] Before then, there were silk brokerages which collected hand-reeled silk and transported it to Guangzhou for export. With the lowered demand for hand-reeled silk, the silk brokerages turned into cocoon brokerages. The brokers sometimes owned, but more often rented, the buildings along with the drying ovens where the cocoons were properly dried prior to sale. In some localities, intermediate brokers acted as middlemen by collecting the cocoons from the farmers and transporting them to the cocoon brokers for a small commission.[19] Shunde County gradually developed into a regional cocoon-marketing center in Guangdong, facilitated by an efficient waterway. Rongqi (容奇) and Guizhou (桂州) in Shunde acted as centers for collecting cocoons and sending them to filatures.[20]

In Shanghai, some filatures continued to send their agents to buy cocoons at the local market, some even owned their own drying ovens, but many purchased cocoons through intermediary brokers. By 1920, no more than 30–40% of cocoons in Jiangnan were sold directly to filatures.[21]

The Decline of the Silk Industry

The silk industry improved the standard of living and brought wealth to the people in the silk-production regions, especially those in the Pearl River Delta Region, which developed into an area with thriving industries of intermediate technology. The silk industry in China reached its peak in the early 1920s.

Even before then, however, problems began to emerge. In both regions, with specialization taking place in different stages of silk production, there was a lack of vertical integration of the industry from mulberry culture to silkworm raising, and silk reeling to silk export. Few farmers engaged in both mulberry cultivation and silkworm rearing. Few filaturists reared silkworms or cultivated mulberry trees. Each stage often involved an intermediary who acted as a supplier of capital or loans to the producer or the buyer, a practice characteristic of rural production and urban handicrafts. To most producers in this system, expansion of volume, cost containment, and the ability to get the goods to the market quickly occupied their minds and quality improvement was hardly thought of. Preoccupation with cost cutting led to a decline in good quality cocoons and an increase in the spread of silkworm disease as breeding practices deteriorated.[22] In the late 1920s and 1930s, it was estimated that about 90% of cocoons in China were affected by disease and nearly 75% silkworms hatched died before reaching the spinning stage. While one pound of good silkworm eggs would yield 110–113 pounds of cocoons before, the same quantity would yield only 15–25 pounds.[23] As cocoon supply accounted for 75% of the cost of production, the profit of the silk industry decreased appreciably.

The government imposed taxes at several levels of the silk industry. The most important was the *likin* (釐金), an internal tariff of the Qing government and the government of the Republic of China.[24] In the Yangtze River Delta area, the cocoon brokerages collected these taxes on behalf of the government and, in turn, were given local monopoly for their services. Carriers of cocoons were often subjected to harassment and extralegal exactions by collectors at the numerous customs stations along the major highways and waterways. In 1883, the *likin* on fresh cocoons was $4 per *picul* and for dried cocoons $12 per *picul*. The regular *likin* for silk was $16 per *picul*, and in 1900, a surcharge of $13 was added to the regular silk *likin* by the Qing government to help pay off the indemnities of the Boxer's Rebellion. To avoid paying the *likin,* some Chinese filatures in Shanghai were registered as foreign firms and they would only have to pay a small fixed transit tax in lieu of *likin* and extralegal payments at the customs stations. In addition, for the Chinese firms, there were other taxes such as user's tax.[25]

In contrast, cocoon carriers in Guangdong were not subjected to harassment as those in Shanghai. The cocoon brokers in Guangdong were merely intermediaries between cocoon sellers and filatures and non-government-licensed monopolists that acted as collection agencies. Nevertheless, in the mid-1920s, *likin* and taxes rose sharply. Cocoons going to Guangzhou from the Xijiang (West River) were subjected to a *likin* of $37 per *picul*, about 2% of the prevailing cocoon price. The raw silk manufacturers paid a *likin* and other taxes totalling $417.5 per *picul* of raw silk with a freight cost of $1.2 per *picul*.[26] The price of raw silk in the world market at that time was around $1,000 per *picul*.[27] The high taxes and *likins* in the late 1920s together with the high cost of cocoons rendered silk production no longer profitable.

The total raw silk exports fell precipitously from an all-time high of 475,000 *piculs* in 1928 to 277,000 *piculs* in 1930, and further to 147,000 *piculs* in 1932. Only 15 out of 107 filatures in Shanghai, 14 out of 49 in Wuxi and fewer than 10 out of 30 in Jiangsu and Zhejiang remained open. At Guangzhou, raw silk exports declined from 81,562 *piculs* in 1931 to 33,862 in 1932 while the number of filatures remained open fell from 111 to 58 during the same period. Even Chen Qiyuan's filature closed its doors in 1928. Total unemployment exceeded 100,000 in Guangzhou in 1932. Figure 1.8 shows the number of filatures operating in Shunde and in Nanhai from 1923–1934, the interval embracing the golden age of the silk industry and its subsequent period of decline.[28]

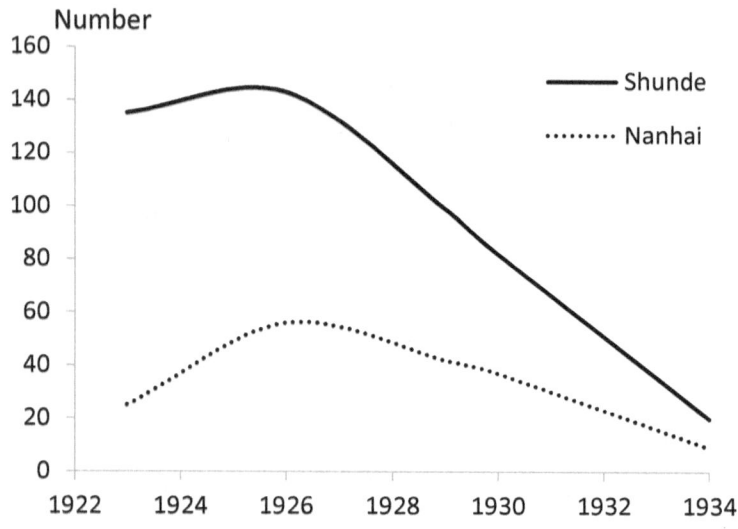

Figure 1.8. Number of filatures in Shunde and Nanhai from 1922 to 1934 (Source: Wong Chor Yee, "Proto-industrialization and the Silk Industry of the Canton Delta, 1664-1934", PhD Thesis, University of Madison–Wisconsin, 1995, 342, Table 4.61)

With the high cost of production and the high taxes and *likins*, the dramatic decline in the demand for raw silk as a result of global depression in the late 1920s and early 1930s, together with the progressive replacement of silk by synthetic textiles such as rayon and nylon, raw silk was no longer an important item of export for China.

During the Japanese invasion of China starting in 1937, the silk-producing regions suffered irreparable damages. Millions of mulberry trees were cut down. Filatures and egg-producing stations were destroyed. The devastation was so extensive and severe that mulberry-leaf production had not recovered to prewar level even in the 1950s. Political events after 1950s did not allow the silk industry to develop until much later because of the Korean War, the United Nations embargo, and other internal turmoil.

Chapter 2: Life in Jiancun, Xiqiao (1836 to 1854)

The Chen Clan

Waves of massive southern migration occurred in China periodically over the centuries, usually caused by hostile invasions from the north or by famine, uprisings, and conflicts between consecutive dynasties that drove the people to find a place where they could settle, live, and raise their children in peace. Chen Qiyuan's ancestor, Chen Guangxian (陳光先), migrated from Longxi County (龍溪鎮) in Fujian Province (福建) to Jiancun (簡村), Xiqiao (西樵), Nanhai (南海) district in Guangdong Province (廣東) during the mass migration that occurred between the Yuan Dynasty and the Ming Dynasty. The family settled in Jiancun during the reign of the first emperor of the Ming Dynasty, Zhu Yuanzhang (朱元璋), in 1390. The village, having derived its name initially from settlement of the Jian (簡) family, received several other families such as Chen (陳), Sin (冼), Li (李), Lin (林), Guo (郭), Mok (莫), and Feng (馮).[1] There were, at the time of Qiyuan's birth, about 2,000 living in the village and over one-third bore the surname Chen.[2] Chen Qiyuan, the seventeenth generation of the Chens in Jiancun, was born in 1836, 446 years after his ancestor Chen Guangxian had settled in Jiancun. There was a dispute as to the year of Qiyuan's birth: 1825 according to

Cihai[3] (辭海) and 1834 according to other sources such as "the Pedigree of the Chen's Clan" (陳啟沅族譜世系表) displayed in the Chan Qiyuan Memorial Hall (Figure 2.1). In this book, 1836 is used as the year of birth and 1904 the year of death, according to the family record.[4]

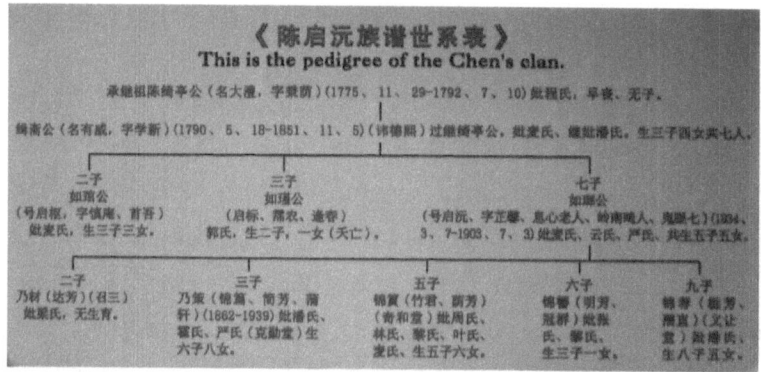

Figure 2.1. Family Tree of Chen Qiyuan from his grandfather to his sons as displayed in Chen Qiyuan Memorial Hall (photo by David Yeung)

Pearl River Delta

Chen Guangxian made a very wise choice to settle in Jiancun of Nanhai County, which is situated on the Zhujiang (珠江, Pearl River) Delta where three rivers, Beijiang (北江, North River), Xijiang (西江, West River), and Dongjiang (東江, East River) merge to form the Pearl River before entering the South China Sea. Although the Pearl River Delta Region is now an economic hub and a major manufacturing center for China and the world, before the 1970s it was mainly dominated by farms and small rural villages. For the most part, the land in the Delta is level with ranges of granite

34

mountain and sandstone hills jutting up from the level plains. It is crisscrossed by a network of tributaries and distributaries of the Pearl River (Figure 2.2). The alluvial soil is unexcelled in richness, unsurpassed in fertility, and water is readily available everywhere. It is one of the most prosperous regions of China, where, in general, two crops of rice and in certain areas up to three, were harvested annually. Specialized farming, such as mulberry cultivation for silkworm rearing with its natural accompaniment, fish culture, was usual in the region. While tea was not raised to a large extent in the Delta, fruits, legumes, and vegetables such as bananas, pineapples, lychees, guava, sugarcane, and peanuts, were plentiful.[5]

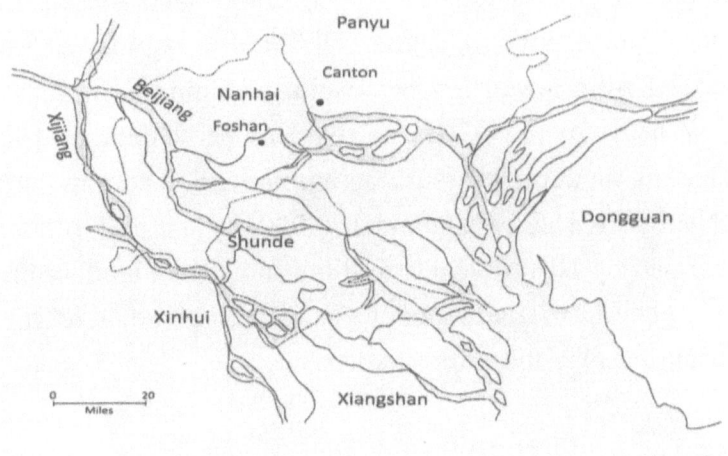

Figure 2.2. Map of the Pearl River Delta showing the numerous waterways in Foshan, Nanhai, Shunde and Dongguan counties (modified from Wong, "Proto-industrialization and the Silk Industry of the Canton Delta, 1662–1934", 109)

For centuries the people in Xiqiao and in the rest of the Pearl River Delta enjoyed a relatively good life, where men farmed and women engaged in all aspects of sericulture, including mulberry culture, silkworm rearing, cocoon production, and silk reeling, all of which provided important bi-employment for women and added to the family income considerably.

The population in China grew during the Qing Dynasty from 198 to 429 million between 1761 and 1850, a sharp gain of 217% in less than a century. The population growth rate was particularly rapid in the Pearl River Delta Region, where it increased from 6.8 million to 28 million, exceeding 400% over the same period. This striking population growth far outstripped arable land for the first time in the history of China. The land-to-population ratio dropped from seven *mu* per capita (1 Chinese *mu* [畝] = 0.167 acre) in the 1760s to two *mu* per capita in 1820, reflecting an acute pressure on arable land. The population in Nanhai in 1662 was about 100,000; by the mid-1850s, it increased by 10-fold to 1.1 million. Individual landholdings were generally small, about two-thirds of an acre for a peasant family, and often smaller.[6]

The Young Qiyuan

Qiyuan was the third son and the youngest child in a family with seven children, three boys and four girls. His older brothers were Qishu (啟樞) who was the second-born, and Qibiao (啟標), the third-born in the family. Qiyuan's father was a merchant before his "retirement" and had saved some money.⁷ After "retirement," his father tilled the land, helped by the two older sons. As it was difficult to feed and clothe such a big family on a small piece of land, sericulture and silk-reeling by the women in the family brought in extra income just like for other families in Xiqiao. Mulberry trees were grown in abundance on the dikes of fish ponds in Nanhai.

It is obvious that Qiyuan's father was more than a farmer. In his book *Can Sang Pu*, (蠶桑譜, *On Sericulture*)⁸, Qiyuan wrote that his father, after "retirement," established a *si-shu* named Le Gengtang (樂耕堂, Joy of Farming, see Figure 2.3), where Qiyuan learned a great deal about the importance of farming. When Qiyuan asked his father to clarify the reasons why farming was so important, his father explained that China was an agrarian society where economy was based on producing crops and maintaining farmland, and that famers should not neglect their duty of tilling the land. His father also quoted Mencius's (孟子) teaching that when the people in an agrarian society learn the methods of growing the five grains: rice, two kinds of millet, wheat, and beans (稻, 黍, 稷, 麥, 豆), and bring about abundant harvests, they could live and raise their children. Likewise, sages such as Emperor Shun (舜帝) and Yi Yin (伊尹), a prime minister of the early Shang Dynasty, found their joy in farming. Who are we not to do so? In an agrarian society, the wealth of the nation depends on the land and hard work of the people who till it. If generations after generations work hard and are proud of what they do, then the nation would become rich and powerful. Confucius had also stated,

"When ordinary people become prosperous, how can the ruler not become affluent?"⁹ Qiyuan's father expounded further:

> In farming, very low investment is required and yet the yield is often hundredfold: one seed of grain can yield hundreds of new grains; one moth can laid eggs capable of giving hundreds of larvae and one larva is capable of producing 3,000 to 4,000 feet of silk; one sweet potato can yield scores of *catties* (斤, one *catty* = 0.6 kg or 1.323 pounds) of new sweet potatoes, provided the farmer sows the seed, waters the plants, applies fertilizer and removes the weeds. Do remember these words.¹⁰

Figure 2.3. The painting of Joy of Farming *si-shu* in Chen Qiyuan Memorial Hall (photo by May Kaan)

The explanation revealed his father's attitude towards people, society, and country, and his classical education and his knowledge on the thoughts of Confucius and Mencius.

38

These words, in turn, imprinted on the young Qiyuan during his impressionable age and molded his attitude towards purpose in life.

When Qiyuan was young, he was the only one spared from the drudgery of farm work. The family left him alone to carry on with his studies. It seems that Qiyuan, the youngest and probably the brightest, carried the hopes of the whole family on his shoulders: to enter the civil service to become a scholar-official of the Qing government by taking part in the Imperial Examination System, a dream of every rural family in China. If successful, the social status of the family would be raised.

Established in the Zhou Dynasty about 3,000 years ago, the Imperial Examination was used to select the best and brightest of the intellectual elite to become government officials. Since anyone could take part in the Imperial Examination, it would permit social mobility and allow some kind of representation from various regions of the country. However, the rigidity of the examination system and the set format of using the "eight-legged essay" (八股文), a style of writing used in the Imperial Examination, stifled original thought and limited the topics prescribed in the examination system, leading to the narrowness of intellectual life and autocratic power of the emperor. It discouraged the Chinese intellectuals from learning mathematics and to conduct experimentation, and hence contributed to China's scientific and economic development trailing way behind Europe.

To qualify for the Imperial Examination, the individual must have succeeded in the "Child Examination" which required him to pass three levels of examination: county examination conducted by the county magistrate, prefectural examination by the prefect, and the provincial examination by the provincial education commissioners. An individual who passed the examination was known as *Shengyuan* (生員), or *Xiucai* (秀才, "Cultivated Talent").

The Imperial Examination itself was also divided into three levels: *Xiāngshì* (鄉試), *Huìshì* (會試), and *Diànshì* (殿試). Once an individual passed the "Child Examination," he could take part in *Xiangshi*, which was held at the provincial capitals once every three years. All attendants must be a *Shengyuan* or *Xiucai*. Those who succeeded in the *Xiangshi* received the *Juren* (舉人, "Recommended Man") status. Only *Jurens* were allowed to take part in *Huìshì*, which was held at the national capital every three years. The examination questions of *Huìshì* were prepared and graded by distinguished capital officials and those who passed were designated as *Gongshi* (貢士, "Tribute Scholar"). All *Gongshi* could take part in *Diànshì*, or palace examination, conducted by the emperor and they were ranked. Those who qualified were called *Jinshi* (進士, "Advanced Scholar") and those in the highest section were admitted to the *Hanlin Academy* (翰林院), where they carried out advanced studies and prepared themselves to become officials of the greatest responsibility and highest rank. The path to civil service was long and arduous, as examinations for each level (except the entry level) were held only once every three years, making competition keen. It is not uncommon for a candidate to take the examination of each level several times before progressing onto a higher level.[11]

Qiyuan had learned by heart all the standard classics, such as the *Three Character Classic* (三字經), the *Thousand Character Classic* (千字文), the *Filial Piety Classic* (孝經), and *Qiushuǐ xuan chidu* (秋水軒尺牘), which were the core curriculum of the "Child Examination."[12] He had also read widely beyond the curriculum for the "Child Examination," such as *Sishu Wujing* (四書五經, *Four Books and Five Classics*), which illustrate the core value and belief systems in Confucian thought, L*unyu* (論語, *Analects of Confucius*), and some of the books such as *Zhuzi baijia* (諸子百家, *Various Sages and Hundred Schools of Thought*),[13] but found himself more interested in other philosophers. Despite his efforts, he failed the "Child Examination" twice.[14]

Qiyuan's failure was not because he did not know the materials in the curriculum, nor because of his lack of intellectual capabilities. With his natural gift of photographic memory, he had no difficulties in reciting these classics by heart. Nevertheless only a few (less than 5%) passed the Imperial Examinations in those days and even fewer received titles.[15] By nature, Qiyuan was not one who would be willing to be restricted and bound to a rigid system. Judging from his later performance in life, Qiyuan possessed a very active enquiring mind, constantly seeking to learn by asking questions and carrying out experiments to prove his hypotheses—a manner in stark contrast to the rigid curriculum of the Imperial Examination System.

Qiyuan loved to fix things in the house and on the farm. Whenever something failed to work, Qiyuan would spend hours taking it apart methodically to identify the problem and, if possible, to remove or replace it and put the parts back together again. In the first half of the nineteenth century, China was a rural country and machines were uncommon except a few such as the silk reeling machines operated by hand and used mostly by the women. Whenever his mother or sisters had problems with their silk reeling machine, they would ask Qiyuan to fix it. Over the years, he became very familiar with the machine.

In the Chen household, there was an unusual piece of furniture, an old pendulum wall clock,[16] brought home from Macau (formerly Macao) by his father some years ago when he was involved in trade. Qiyuan would sit by the clock and stare at the pendulum swinging to-and-fro, to-and-fro, mesmerized by the tick-tock, tick-tock sound. He marveled at the regularity and precision of its motion and loved the sound made by the striking of the clock every quarter-hour and on the hour. He noted that when the tick-tock sound was offbeat, the clock became inaccurate, and he learned that adjusting it to make sure that it was level corrected the inaccuracy. He also learned from his father that since ancient times people judged the time of day by looking at the shadow of a stationary object cast by the sun, the sundial. It was invented to tell time by displaying the position of a shadow on a flat surface which has markings that correspond to the hour.

One day the old wall clock turned silent. It had stopped working. There was no one in the village who knew how to fix it. After all, a clock in those days was a luxury item, and most unusual to have in a village. For the village folks, timekeeping was not necessary or important for rural economy. Qiyuan gathered his courage and asked permission from his father whether he could open it to find out what went wrong. He meticulously took the clock apart, putting down the parts removed in order and examining them carefully. A pendulum clock has several parts: 1) a weight on a chain that turns a pulley; 2) a gear train that divides the rotation rate to turn wheels that rotate once every hour and once every 12 hours to turn the hands of the clock; 3) a metal bar (escapement) that gives the pendulum precisely-timed impulses to keep it swinging and to release the gear train wheels to move forward a fixed amount at each swing; 4) the pendulum, a weight on a rod, which is the timekeeping element of the clock; and 5) the clock face with rotating hands that record how much time has passed.

Qiyuan examined all the parts carefully with his penetrating eyes and did not detect any defects, but he noticed that the clock was old and the gear train rusty. He placed the gear train in kerosene and cleaned it thoroughly. He also cleaned the other parts of the clock. After applying machinery oil to lubricate the moving parts, he carefully reassembled the parts in reverse order, something that he had done so many times with the hand silk reeling machines. And the clock came back to life, working perfectly. The tick-tock sound returned. He then checked its accuracy against the homemade sundial. Qiyuan was proud of himself for fixing the clock.

Qiyuan was endowed with a very special gift: he was able to see things very far away for which ordinary people would require a telescope, and to see very small things that others would require a powerful magnifying glass or a microscope. However, he was not eager to show off his special talent.

His keenness to learn new things, to find out how they work, and to identify their problems when they fail to work and how to fix them was certainly not encouraged or appreciated in the Imperial Examination curriculum but would be important in science and technology. This trait, together with his love of mathematics, his proficiency in the use of the abacus (the traditional Chinese calculator), his gift of unusually powerful eyesight, and perseverance all contributed to his success in life.

Unequal Foreign Treaties and Domestic Uprisings

The peaceful, sleepy village life of Jiancun did not last long for Qiyuan. For centuries, Chinese dynasties, especially the Ming and Qing (1368–1911 CE), had regarded their country as the center of the world. During the Song Dynasty (960–1279 CE), China was the country in the world with the most advanced technology—the Chinese people had invented printing, paper money, gunpowder, and the compass. During the Ming Dynasty, China was a world leader in gunpowder-based weaponry, shipbuilding, and the production of porcelain. Over the centuries, countries that wanted to have any type of relationship with China—political, economic or otherwise—had to partake in the tribute system. The Chinese emperors and their courts were accustomed to peripheral countries arriving and paying tribute to them. During Emperor Zhu Di's (朱棣) reign in the Ming Dynasty, Zheng He (鄭和), a fleet admiral and court eunuch, using the most innovative shipbuilding and sailing technology of the time, conducted seven sea voyages on behalf of the emperor to trade and to collect tributes in the eastern Pacific and Indian Oceans.

Things changed in an opposite direction after the death of Zheng He in 1433; the next emperor discontinued all sea voyages. Instead, the Ming Dynasty initiated a strict ban on trade with foreigners at sea. This policy of seclusion persisted into the Qing Dynasty era. They had in place two great physical barriers: in the north, over ten thousand miles of the Great Wall to protect themselves from invasions of the barbarians and along the vast Chinese coastline, and a system of patrol and communication linked by "fire beacon" towers (烽火臺), built in various strategic locations, using smoke signals by day and fire at night to prevent the invasion of the pirates mostly from Japan.[17] These two measures had been used by Chinese emperors for some 3,000 years.

Despite the barriers at sea, the Portuguese in 1557 managed to secure an outpost in Macau and started directing maritime trade between Europe and China. Trade accelerated after the Spanish conquest of the Philippines. In 1573, the sea route for trade was established between Europe, Mexico, and China, with the Philippines as the nexus, where white silver from Mexico was exchanged for tea, silk, and porcelain from China.[18] Gradually the British Royal Navy replaced the Spanish fleet to become the overlord at sea. Due to its position in India and the strength of the British Royal Navy, the British East India Company came to dominate Sino-European trade.

Guangzhou became the first port of call for most Europeans because of its geographic position at the mouth of the Pearl River. Since 1700, Guangzhou became the center of maritime trade when foreigners were no longer allowed to enter and do business in any other ports in China.[19] The demand for tea, porcelain, and silk from the Europeans seemed insatiable. But the Chinese were self-sufficient and did not require any manufactured goods from the West, creating a trade imbalance between the Qing government and the British government. As a result, European silver flowed into China in huge quantities. To address the imbalance, British merchants finally found something that the Chinese wanted: opium, which was transported to the Chinese coast where local middlemen made massive profits selling it in China. The amount of opium imported into China increased dramatically and reversed the trade surplus and drained the silver from the Chinese economy and treasury. In the meantime, Chinese people, rich and poor alike, gathered in opium dens called divans to smoke the drug. Millions of Chinese—government officials, merchants, coolies and servants—became addicted and subdued.[20]

As the Chinese consumption of opium grew, Emperor Jiaqing (嘉慶) became alarmed and banned opium trade in 1799, but the ban was easily circumvented by British merchants, who involved greedy and corrupt Chinese local officials in the smuggling network.[21] In 1839, Emperor Daoguang (道光) appointed Viceroy Lin Zexu (林則徐) to oversee the ban. Lin confiscated around 20,000 chests (about 1,210 tons or 2.66 million sterling pounds) of opium from the British merchants without offering compensation and ordered the blockade of opium trade in Guangzhou. The British objected to this unexpected seizure and dispatched a military force to China. In the ensuing conflict, the British Royal Navy, using its superior naval and gunnery power, defeated the Qing government.

In 1842, The Qing government was forced to sign the Nanjing (Nanking) Treaty, the first of a series of unequal treaties. The treaty included the cession of Hong Kong to Britain and the opening of five other treaty ports where the British could reside and enjoy extraterritorial rights, monetary compensation for the destroyed opium and the British properties, and the granting of British merchants the most favored status with the Qing government.[22] Tariffs were limited to 5% and inland transit dues on foreign goods imported into the interior or on Chinese goods for export were limited to a nominal charge. In addition, the Maritime Customs Office and the Salt Administration came under foreign management.[23] The crucial problem of opium was never addressed.[24]

The humiliating defeat of the Qing government had a great deal to do with inferior weaponry and poor technology. China had trailed far behind in science and technology development and had not become as industrialized as in Western countries. China had isolated itself from the Western world for centuries. Successive emperors and ruling mandarins, accustomed to nearby countries paying tributes to them, carried the complacent and arrogant attitude that there was nothing new and worthwhile to learn from "barbarians," and a delusion that their country was the most advanced in the world. Following Renaissance, science and technology advanced by leaps and bounds in Europe. The invention of the steam engine in 1781 by James Watt in Britain and its application to supply power for industries heralded the Industrial Revolution in Britain and other Western countries. With steam energy, the West, especially Britain, produced a great deal more manufactured goods than they needed and had to aggressively find markets to export their goods. China seemed to possess the potential for a huge and desirable market.

The Qing government also faced internal threats of social unrest and revolts. The population of China exploded while the land remained stagnant.[25] From the early to mid-nineteenth century the country was haunted by a series of natural disasters, droughts, floods, and famines, for which the Qing government was unable to provide any effective relief. Heavy taxes and rents imposed on farmers to pay compensation to Britain, one of the sequelae of the First Opium War, led the farmers to desert their land in droves.

They became bandits, or members of secret societies. As the Qing government, led by the inapt Manchu, became increasingly corrupt, antigovernment sentiments swelled in many parts of the country.[26]

The most important uprising was the Taiping Rebellion led by Hong Xiuquan (洪秀全), a Hakka, who claimed to be the younger brother of Jesus Christ. He and his followers established the God-Worshipping Society (拜上帝會), seeking to convert Chinese people to the Taiping version of Christianity and to overthrow the Qing Government. In 1851, Taiping rebels took up arms and drove Qing government forces out of Jintian (金田), Guangxi. Hong declared himself the Emperor of Taiping Heavenly Kingdom (太平天國). The Taiping forces fought their way along the mid- and lower Yangtze Valley, and in 1853, they seized Nanjing and made it the capital of the Taiping Heavenly Kingdom. Over the next 14 years, the Taiping Army marched through many provinces in China. Beijing, the capital of the Qing government, was also threatened at one point. The Qing Army was at a loss as to how to tackle the Taiping rebels. In the end, plagued by internal conflicts, the Taipings were defeated by local militias: the Xiang Army (湘軍) founded by Zeng Guofan (曾國藩) in Hunan, the Huai Army (淮軍) founded by Li Hongzhang (李鴻章) in Anhui, and the Ever-Victorious Army (常勝軍) led by General Charles G. Gordon and organized by foreign merchants in Shanghai. Nanjing was retaken in 1864 and the Taiping Heavenly Kingdom ended with the suicide of Hong Xiuquan. The Taiping Rebellion was the most bloody civil war recorded in the history of the world because up to 70 million were killed and as high as 100 million were displaced.[27]

During the Taiping Rebellion, life in villages, including Jiancun, deteriorated. Since the signing of the Nanjing Treaty, more and more foreign goods arrived even at the village level. Products for everyday use, such as matches, soap, cloth, and candles, were particularly popular and purchased by ordinary people as they were inexpensive and of better quality compared to domestic products. The prevalence of foreign imports destroyed the local cottage industry and the bi-employment of women at home. Hunger and unemployment drove the rural people to join the Taiping Rebellion.

Closer to home, San Ho Hui (三合會, Triple Union Society, referring to the union of Heaven, Earth and Man) under Chen Hai (陳海) organized an uprising in Foshan (佛山) in 1854. Within days, over 10,000 people joined the uprising from nearby counties. They sieged Guangzhou for over six months but ultimately lost to the Qing army. The rebels, who survived scattered, changed their names and settled in different villages, even in Jiancun. Aroused by the fascinating and passionate stories told by these people, Qiyuan briefly toyed with the idea of joining such groups to fight for the betterment of the lives of people.[28]

An Uncertain Future

The situation also worsened at home. In 1851, at the age of 15, Qiyuan lost his father.[29] Following the usual route of those who had failed the Imperial Examination, and there had been-quite a few in Nanhai, Qiyuan became a teacher at Joy of Farming Si-shu to assist his oldest brother, Qishu, to make ends meet. Qishu had replaced his father as the family's breadwinner. Between the two of them, they only brought in 20 to 30 *taels* of silver each year from about eight to 10 students (one *tael* of silver equaled 1,000 copper coins and one egg cost about two to three copper coins). Because the cost of food for one individual was around five *taels* of silver per year, the income from the *si-shu* was hardly adequate for the whole family.[30] The number of students also decreased progressively as the villagers could no longer afford to send their children to school.[31]

During this period the Chen family was rapidly expanding—Qishu had married and had several children in rapid succession. As the amount of food dwindled on the table, everyone became concerned. To earn some extra money, Qiyuan sold oil in the village apart from teaching in the *si-shu* and helping with farm work. In one particularly chilly winter, when food was scarce, they had no rice and had to survive on sweet potatoes. Qiyuan was seen retrieving a sweet potato that he dropped into a stream by accident. He quickly dried it and ate it. He was seen eating sweet potatoes so often that he earned the nickname "Sweet Potato Yuan" from the villagers.[32]

In desperation, Qishu, unable to feed his wife and children, sent them to his wealthy father-in-law, Mr. Mak (麥). The Maks were a large well-to-do-family with many relatives living and working in Annam (a name synonymous with Vietnam until 1945). Mr. Mak advised Qishu to go to Annam to work with one of his relatives and to make a life for himself and his family. In the meantime, he would look after his daughter and grandchildren.[33] This advice changed the life not only of Qishu but also of the whole Chen family, particularly Qiyuan.

With Qishu gone, Qibiao (啟標), the second son (third-born) in the Chen family, became the master of Joy of Farming Si-shu. Young Qiyuan continued to teach at the Si-shu and help with the farm work. He kept up his studies of classical texts and the works of other philosophers, writers, mathematicians, and astronomers. When he turned 16, he had to seriously think about what to do with his life and his future, bearing in mind the precarious situation of his country with threats both internally and externally. But what could he do? Not being the military type, he could only be in the civil service for his country. After the failure in the "Child Examination" twice, he was no longer eager to pursue the path of becoming a scholar-official. Should he follow his father's footsteps of becoming a half-farmer and half-scholar? Would he be able to feed his family? What about becoming a merchant, just like his father when he was young? This would certainly lower the family's social status—the hierarchy of social order in China was scholar, farmer, artisan, and merchant as the lowest ranking occupation. Being a practical person, he had no qualms about being a merchant, for if he could become wealthy, he would be able to feed his family and help the poor people in the village.

52

In 1854, Qishu returned to Jiancun after three years to visit family, as customary for emigrants if they could afford it, bringing excitement to the whole household. Qishu's sojourn in Annam had been more than successful. Employed initially in a general store of a relative of Mr. Mak, his ability to read and write, his skill with the abacus, and his hard work and honesty earned him the trust of his employer. He was given the responsibility of supervising a building project. He completed the project so well that the employer gave him a big bonus, a significant percentage of the profit of the project, in addition to his regular wage. Even though he had been sending his earnings home regularly, with this huge bonus, Qishu could start a small business of his own in Annam, an undertaking that would necessitate the help of another person.[34]

Cholon (堤岸), where Qishu worked, was developing rapidly then as the Vietnamese government expanded the country southward. After several days of intensive discussions, the brothers decided that instead of dividing the family assets, the family should stay together and work towards a common goal. Qiyuan would go and help Qishu in Annam. Qibiao, being older, would take up the responsibility of looking after the entire family in Jiancun and tending to the farm. The earnings from the farm and those from Annam would be divided into three equal portions. Money would be remitted regularly to supplement the income at home. The brothers and their families kept the agreement until more than 30 years later.[35]

Chinese Emigrants

Despite the strict closure of the coastline with ban on sea trade and the 1712 imperial edict that forbade Chinese from leaving their homeland without special permits, along with the threat of the death penalty on those who violated the law, Chinese have ventured abroad to trade over the centuries.[36] But few ever settled permanently in their new environment, and they almost always returned home upon retirement. Ancestral worship, family ties, filial piety, and love of their native villages made these emigrants sojourners.

Emigrants usually came from coastal provinces such as Guangdong and Fujian. They travelled in junks along the coast of China to different parts of Southeast Asia. Many landed in Annam at that time. The numbers were, in general, not large. It was not until the latter half of the nineteenth century that the number of Chinese emigrants escalated, and their destinations increased and varied widely to different parts of the world. The pressure on land from the rising population, the poor economy, the unrest, and the declining power of the Qing Dynasty since the First Opium War led to an unprecedented outflow of Chinese emigrants. At the same time, with the abolition of slave trade in the British Empire in 1807 and later in other European countries, the demand for free labor seemed limitless. The Europeans (English, Dutch, and French) had founded settlements in their colonies and turned to China for cheap manual labor to accomplish their exploitation. In the unequal treaties, they forced China to yield to their demands. In 1860, coolie trade became legalized for the first time in the Peking Covenant.[37] Many

Chinese were recruited to work in different plantations through the indenture or contract system and the credit-ticket system. The recruiters went to villages and used various methods to entice men, and later bound them by written agreement to work for a fixed number of years in a foreign land. Their sea passage was paid and later deducted from their wages over a period of years together with interest. Under another system, the credit-ticket, the brokers provided transportation and paid the expenses of the emigrant who had no political protection or capital. They had to work for a number of years to pay off their debt and were exploited and abused during the period when their obligations were not yet met. One other method of emigration was assistance from relatives and friends either at home or abroad.

From 1848 to 1870, Macau was a transit port of coolie trade for southern China. Some of emigrants were kidnapped from Guangdong Province and were shipped off in packed vessels to Cuba, Peru, or other South American countries.[38] After 1870, most emigrants would use the well-protected harbor of Hong Kong, an island at the mouth of the Pearl River Delta which became a British colony in 1842, as the stepping-stone for their emigration.[39]

Voyage to Annam

When Qiyuan turned 18, his mother insisted that he should be married. Before he left, he was delighted to learn that his wife was pregnant. With a heavy heart, he left his wife and his unborn child, even though he knew that his mother and his family would look after her well. He had no idea of what to expect in Annam, but he was determined to work hard and do his very best to be successful in business so that he would be able to achieve his aim of relieving the poverty of his family and his village.

With Qishu, Qiyuan began his journey to Annam in the summer of 1854, paying their own passage without the use of a broker or agent, as Qishu by then could afford the passage for them both. The journey took them to Macau rather than Hong Kong, which had not yet developed into an important immigration center. From Macau, the brothers embarked on a Chinese junk which headed southwest to Cholon along the coastline. As the Chinese junk sailed, Qiyuan caught sight of the coastline, which appeared as a long green line with gray-blue hills behind it. The water was dark blue, and the light shimmered in the water. Occasionally seagulls circled above them, and fishes broke water creating a splendid sight. The first five days at sea were peaceful and calm, and mild heat was relieved by the gentle breeze.

While he enjoyed these wonderful scenes, Qiyuan made full use of these days by seeking information of the Vietnamese people and their customs from his brother and at the same time learning a few phrases of Vietnamese so that he would be able to communicate and get around in Cholon. Fascinated by the speed with which the junk surged ahead even with just a gentle breeze in the calm sea, he asked the crew about how the sails worked. He learned that the structure and flexibility of the junk sails enabled the junk to sail fast and be easily controlled. The sails include several horizontal bars, called "battens," which provide shape and strength to the sails. The battens also make the sails more resistant to large tears. The sails of a junk can be moved inward toward the long axis of the ship and allow the junk to sail into the wind. In principle, the junk sails have much in common with the aerodynamically efficient sails used today in windsurfing sails or catamarans. The Chinese junk has been considered by historian Herbert Warington Smyth to possess one of the most efficient ship designs.[40]

Qiyuan learned from the crew that they used the compass for navigation. Before the discovery of the compass, people depended on celestial bodies at night. They measured the angle between a celestial body such as Polaris (the north polar star), the moon, or one of the other navigational stars and the visible horizon, to identify the position of the ship at sea. All this information he treasured and filed in his memory. At night, Qiyuan lay on the deck and looked at the millions of stars dotted on the vast black sky. They were of different size and shape, blinking and flickering away. He learned how to identify Polaris by locating first the two pointer stars of the Big Dipper (Dubhe and Merak) and the Little Dipper. This keenness in learning, despite no longer a scholar, remained with him all his life.

On the seventh day at sea, dark and forbidding clouds gathered and the wind gradually blew stronger and pushed against the ship. The waves rocked the ship so much that many passengers retched. Then the rain poured. It was in late August, the typhoon season. The captain told everyone to return to the cabin below or else face the danger of being picked up by a gust of wind and flung out to the sea. He added that he would try his best to stay on the southwesterly course and to keep as close to the coastline as possible, but he would have to unload some of the cargo if too much water came into the ship.

The ship rode up and down the mighty swelling sea, and torrential rain fell at intervals. As the condition worsened, the captain announced that the ship could no longer keep the course, and if it hit the reef, it might break up and sink. He continued to say that it would be much safer if he tried to land the ship on a beach, and when that happened, all the passengers must try to find their way towards the land as quickly as possible.

Soon they heard the captain shout that he sighted a white sandy beach, and everyone should be prepared to jump off the ship. A huge wave sent the ship forward and landed it firmly on the beach. Qishu and Qiyuan had been anxiously waiting for this moment. They jumped into the water carrying each his own case and tried to make their way towards land. Suddenly a gigantic wave pushed them forward. While thoroughly soaked wet, they were thankful to be alive.

They landed not too far away from Cholon along the coast of Vietnam. They walked toward south for about 300 kilometers after purchasing some food, cooking utensils, and a good pair of shoes from local villages. After two weeks, they arrived in Cholon uneventfully to start a new life, and for Qiyuan, in a new place as well.[41]

Chapter 3: Years in Vietnam (1854 to 1872)

China and Vietnam

The Chen brothers reached Cholon, a satellite town of Saigon (now Ho Chi Minh City), South Vietnam, in 1854.[1] If they had arrived 1,000 years earlier, they would still be Chinese citizens and not immigrants to Vietnam. Vietnam had been part of the Chinese Imperial Empire since the Han Dynasty during the reign of Emperor Wuti (漢武帝, 140–87 BCE) until the end of the Tang Dynasty, when Chinese rule ended. During 1,000 years of Chinese rule, Vietnam had undergone the process of sinicization of varying intensity and was exposed to Confucianism, Buddhism, and numerous Chinese classics. Yet Vietnam never lost its national consciousness.

In 972 CE, Vietnam gained independence, but it still acknowledged China as its suzerain state. Despite its independence, the Vietnamese rulers kept the essential Chinese forms of social and political structures. In 1883, France captured Hue (順化) and Vietnam was forced to acknowledge France as its protector. Because Vietnam was a vassal state of China, the Qing Court intervened. Although the Qing Army defeated the French in Lang Son (諒山) in 1885, for some unknown reason the Qing government

59

recognized France as the protector of Vietnam. In 1945, after the Second World War, Vietnam declared its independence.[2]

Because of proximity, immigration of Chinese to Vietnam had gone on throughout the centuries. After Vietnam gained its sovereignty, the country became a place of refuge for Chinese dissenters. During periods of unrest and political upheaval in China, waves of Chinese arrived in Vietnam.

Until the eighteenth century there were only a few Chinese merchants who ventured abroad because of the government's policy of banning maritime trade since the Ming Dynasty. The spirit of filial devotion and teachings of Confucius which demanded the unification of families was another major hindrance to Chinese leaving home, and one of the primary reasons for them to return home as soon as they had saved sufficient money. It was not until after the mid-nineteenth century that the Chinese remained permanently in Vietnam to a large extent.[3]

In the fifteenth century, Vietnam consisted mainly of the land around the Red River Valley and a narrow coastal strip running down to between the sixteenth and seventeenth parallels. As the population had been increasing over the years, in the eighteenth century the Vietnamese emperor, Minh Mang, decided to expand the country southwards. He astutely introduced legislation enabling the Chinese to establish settlements in Cochinchina and the Mekong Delta in the southern part of Vietnam. The Chinese, who came mostly from Guangdong, Fujian, and Yunnan as well as Hainan Island, played a major role in developing the first cities and commercial centers in South Vietnam, and in particular, lower Cochinchina.[4]

Figure 3.1. Map of Vietnam and neighboring countries in the nineteenth century. Kampuchea is now Cambodia

Cholon, Tai-Ngon, Saigon, Ho Chi Minh City

Cholon, where the Chen brothers began their business, is currently a district in Ho Chi Minh City, Vietnam. It lies on the west bank of the Saigon River, with Binh Tay Market as its central market. Cholon was first settled in 1778 by the Chinese living in Bien Hoa (邊和市) (Figure 3.1). Because of their support for the Nguyen lords, they were persecuted by the Tay Son forces. The Chinese moved to what was Cholon and built high embankments against the flows of the river and called their new settlement Tai-Ngon (堤岸) or "Embankment." Despite the hardships that they faced, the unabated activity, hard work, and perseverance of the Chinese people developed Tai-Ngon into the most important commercial center of lower Cochinchina. The Vietnamese called it Cholon, meaning "big market."[5] In 1931, Cholon and Saigon were merged to form a single city, Saigon-Cholon. Cholon was dropped from the city's official name in 1956.

When the Chen brothers arrived in Cholon in 1854, Cochinchina had the highest percentage of Chinese in Vietnam and the largest Chinatown, in terms of area, in the world. In 1868, it was estimated that the city of Cholon had 10,600 Chinese and 32,000 Vietnamese. With a floating population of 8,000, the total population approached approximately 50,000.[6] The city was expanding rapidly with more Chinese migrating into the area because of unrest and poverty at home.[7] Cholon had become the storehouse of Cochinchina. From Cholon, goods and commodities were shipped to Singapore, Hong Kong, Batavia, and Bangkok.

Charles Lemire, the French colonial administrator in Saigon-Cholon in 1865, at the same time Qiyuan was in Cholon, gave a vivid description of the wide range of goods and services available and the unusual taste of the people at that time:

> Next door to the undertaker is a merchant of trinkets who sells false hair because if coquetry has been lost in France, we may still find it here in Cochinchina. Further along the road, we find a pharmacist, a barber, and under an awning a pastry confectioner; then a gambling house, a dying workshop, an opium den, a goldsmith's shop and a large store selling manufactured goods from Europe.
>
> Cholon also has a crocodile park. The Annamites are very fond of the flesh of the saurian, which abounds in the arroyos of Cochinchina. In 1865, more than 500 crocodiles from the great Cambodia River were consumed here in Cholon.[8]

Qishu quickly found a place for them to stay temporarily in Cholon. While the possibilities for trade in this thriving city appeared to be enormous, their immediate task was to identify the kind of business that would bring in a reasonable profit with only a small capital from Qishu's savings. The brothers spent the next few days exploring the city to assess the local situation and determine where to set up their shop.

They were attracted to the famous Cholon City Market, which was then a temporary structure. On the riverfront (a branch of the Saigon River), there were rows of major Chinese trading houses and warehouses containing rice, sugar, indigo, wax, silk porcelain, pottery, dried fish, cotton, and peanuts, along with hides of buffalo, oxen, snakes, and tiger. Clerks and porters would congregate around sets of weighing scales and bales of goods of all shapes and sizes.

The Chen brothers were delighted to encounter a familiar sight, the Tin Hau Temple (天后廟), commonly known as the Apocheon Temple (阿婆廟)[9] (Figure 3.2). Next to it was a school sponsored by the temple. In order to maintain and promote Chinese culture, the Chinese established schools, halls, and temples in Ho Chi Minh City, and Tin Hau Temple is one of them. It was built around 1800s but remained well preserved due to renovations over time and is one of the oldest buildings with historical and cultural value in Ho Chi Minh City.

Figure 3.2. Tin Hau or Apocheon Temple, Cholon in 1963 (courtesy of Mr. Fung Yee Wang)

They walked into the temple which covered a wide area. On either side of the entrance stood a pair of majestic stone lions of about 50 years old. The walls and ceiling were elaborately decorated with carvings of birds and dragons, flowers and trees, and green bricks and tiles. There were also big bronze bells cast in the sixtieth year (1795) of the reign of Qing Emperor Qianlong (乾隆). The temple was dedicated to Mazu (媽祖), or Apo (阿婆) and also enshrined some familiar folk heroes. Here the Chen brothers could offer their sacrifices to the merciful goddess to protect their family from danger.

Business Ventures in Annam

First Venture: Junhezhan Grocery Store (均和棧雜貨店)

After several days of research into the market situation, the Chen brothers decided that a grocery store to sell every day necessities like oil, salt, firewood, rice, vinegar, and tea would be of the greatest help to the local residents, and they hoped it would be a business that would have the highest probability of earning their living. They rented a small place which served as a shop during daytime and their bedroom at night. The small courtyard at the back became the kitchen. After spending a small sum on renovation, they began to stock up on the above items with the exception of rice and firewood, which were space occupying. They added matches, tobacco, paper, and other items to their supplies. They called it Junhezhan Grocery Store (均和棧雜貨店).[10]

Because of the shop's convenient central location and most of the goods were everyday necessities, a constant stream of customers was attracted from the neighborhood. Qishu, having lived in Cholon for three years previously, had friends to help identify the sources of supply of goods. His ability to speak Vietnamese proved most useful as he could bargain for quality goods at a relatively inexpensive price. Qiyuan, having learned a few phrases of Vietnamese, looked after sales and cooked the two meals. After a couple of months, they were happy to find that they were not only able to feed themselves, pay the rent, and purchase the goods, but also to make a small profit. More important to them, however, was that they had a home base.[11]

The Second Project: Clocks and Watches Repair

The second business utilized Qiyuan's talent of problem solving, superb eyesight, and dexterous fingers. One day, Qishu mentioned to his brother that he visited his former employer's home in Cholon. There was a beautiful longcase (or grandfather) clock in his employer's living room but it was not working. A gift from a French business colleague, the clock had traveled all the way from Paris. When set up, it disappointingly failed to make the tick-tock sound. They had asked around, but no one in Cholon had the expertise of repairing such a grand instrument. They were thinking of transporting the clock to Saigon for repair even though there was no guarantee that it could be restored. Qiyuan had a knack for fixing mechanical things. At home he had repaired silk reeling machines whenever they were out of order, and on one occasion, he even fixed the pendulum wall clock at home. A grandfather clock is also a pendulum clock and probably more complicated than the wall clock, but the principle should be the same. Tantalized by challenge and curiosity, Qiyuan asked his brother whether he could visit his former employer's home and examine the clock and try to fix it. He might not be able to repair it, but promised that he would not damage it in any way.[12]

Qiyuan spent the following day getting the necessary tools before going to his brother's former employer's home. It was a magnificent grandfather clock, about seven feet tall with an elaborately carved ornamentation on the hood, which surrounded the dial. The pendulum was long, one meter in length. Qiyuan found that the clock was driven by two weights, each suspended by a cable: one driving the pendulum and the other the striking mechanism. Each cable was wrapped around a pulley mounted to the top of each weight. The clock was wound once a week by pulling on the end of each chain, lifting the weights until they came to under the clock's face. Just like the old wall clock at home, it had an anchor escapement mechanism which reduced the swing and caused less friction and wear on the moving parts.

He moved the pendulum; there was no tick-tock sound. He examined the parts to find out whether there was anything that might have prevented the pendulum from moving and noticed that the two pallets of the anchor were not touching the escape wheel at all (Figure 3.3). The anchor had been pushed back, presumably during transportation from Paris. Qiyuan gently pushed the anchor mechanism in place to engage the escape wheel. He pushed the pendulum again, now it made the tick-tock noise, but not regularly. He examined the swing of the pendulum again to find out whether it was touching anything and checked the hands of the dial to make sure that they did not touch each other or the glass case. He checked the cables carefully to see whether they rubbed against each other or got pinched. The hands were quite free. Seeing that everything seemed to be in order, he began to adjust the level of the clock until the tick-tock sound became regular.

Figure 3.3. Anchor escapement in a pendulum clock. The movement of the pendulum is limited by the two pallets of the anchor on the escape wheel below (https://en.wikipedia.org/wiki/Pendulum_clock#/media /File:Anchor_escapement_animation_217x328px.gif)

He then sat and watched the clock for one hour to see whether it chimed correctly with the time. It did. As the clock was new, he did not think cleaning was necessary. But he wanted to check the accuracy of the clock. For this he created a home-made sundial just as he had done at home. After three days of checking at noon time, he found the clock accurate.

Delighted with the result, the owner paid Qiyuan handsomely. Would Qiyuan be willing to fix clocks for his friends as well? The following day, a wall clock was delivered to Qiyuan's shop for repair. After examining it, he could find nothing wrong. He then decided that he should clean and lubricate the parts. After lubrication, the clock ran perfectly. He checked the accuracy of the clock on three successive days before returning it to the owner.[13]

His meticulous workmanship led to increasing demand for his repair services of watches and clocks. Junhezhan Grocery Store became a congested and bustling place. Qiyuan and his brother decided to open another shop specifically devoted to watch and clock repair. However, some preparatory work was required. The two brothers closed the store and spent a couple of days in Saigon, which was then a bigger city with better facilities. Again, they divided the tasks at hand. Qiyuan would find ways to acquire and improve his skills on watch and clock repair and buy the necessary equipment. Qishu would scout around Saigon to assess the current market cost of repair as well as to buy spare parts.

Using his gift of superior vision and a photographic memory, Qiyuan developed a way of acquiring new knowledge. He could see how the repair was done at some distance if there was nothing to obstruct his vision. In the repair shops he asked questions about clocks but kept his eyes on those cloks that were being repaired. At times he positioned himself outside the shop and pretended that he was talking to someone else or reading something, when he was really watching the repair being carried out inside. After a couple of days of observation, he felt that he had seen enough to enable him to tackle a wide range of problems in watches and clocks.

On returning to Cholon, he embarked on the new business venture and put up a sign outside their shop, "Chenji Watches and Clocks Repair Expert" (陳記精修鐘表). At that time, most of the clocks were imported from France and were expensive. Since timekeeping became increasingly important in the business community, clocks were no longer just a piece of fashionable furniture, they were necessities. As more people became affluent, they could afford to buy clocks and watches. Qiyuan's business boomed. He hired a young man and taught him how to remove, clean, and lubricate the parts of clocks and watches carefully while Qiyuan himself would be responsible for reassembling them. Soon he had to hire and train another assistant.[14]

Qiyuan established several rules for his "apprentices:" they must 1) be polite and provide excellent services to customers; 2) ensure the quality of repair (the clocks should be checked for accuracy against another clock for three successive days and the differences should not be greater than three minutes each day); 3) take time to explain

70

carefully to the customer when no spare parts were available for the clock to be repaired; and 4) try their best to identify the problem of a customer's clock and to fix it especially if the clock was brought in a second time for the same problem after it had been fixed.

At six months into the new business, Qiyuan reviewed the situation. The business required little capital investment and had been profitable so far. The repair work was repetitive and did not require great skill most of the time, but the work had to be carried out meticulously and with great care. His attitude of providing excellent service and his honesty brought him numerous customers. Despite his success, Qiyuan did not believe that the increase in business volume would go on forever simply because most clocks and watches were made to last for a long time, two to three decades. The business would eventually slow down, limited by the size and the rate of increase in the local population.[15]

Hard work and prudent spending brought in a profit of 300 *taels* of silver at the end of the first year—their first pot of gold—from their two shops. They sent home 60 *taels* of silver, 20 for each family to support their daily needs.[16] While delighted with the results, they felt that now with more capital at their disposal, they could explore other business opportunities.

The Third Undertaking: Sauce Production

Once again, the two brothers put their heads together and researched the market situation. They used their usual criteria to select a new venture: a small capital investment with a good return and a product fulfilling the need of the local people. There were already retail and wholesale businesses for all the daily necessities for the local populace: firewood, rice, oil, salt, sauce, vinegar, and tea. But popular Chinese sauces, such as soy sauce and other bean sauces and pastes, vital for delicious food making, were hard to come by in Cholon and Saigon then, and the quality was generally poor. Since Qiyuan had hired another assistant for watch and clock repair, he could devote his time to investigate the secrets of sauce making. People in Jiancun had always made soy sauce themselves, and if they could do it, he should be able to do it, too.

He searched and wrote home for recipes for making soy sauce and other types of bean sauces such as ground soybean sauce, black bean sauce, and other fermented bean sauces or pastes that Chinese were fond of. He purchased the necessary equipment and ingredients for making soy sauce first: a large container to soak the beans, a large pot to cook them, a few large, shallow, four-inch deep baskets, and a 50-gallon earthenware jar, soybeans, yeast, salt, and wheat flour. The small backyard of the repair shop became his laboratory. Following the instructions carefully, Qiyuan first washed the soybeans and soaked them in water for over 12 hours. He drained off excess water from the beans and cooked them for several hours. He added wheat flour to the cooked soybeans using the ratio of about three pounds of wheat flour to 10 pounds of cooked soybeans, mixed the beans and flour, and then inoculated the mixture with yeast and mold. The inoculation culture was made by growing the mold on steamed rice. After this, he spread the mash in a layer three inches deep in the baskets. The baskets were then stacked carefully in such a way so that air would circulate freely over the beans. During this stage, considerable heat was given off. After three days, Qiyuan detected a thin, white surface growth of mold, which soon turned yellow with spore growth. He put this molded soy-wheat mash into the deep earthenware vessel and covered the mash with 20% brine. The earthenware vessel was placed in the open air and covered only when it rained. He stirred the mixture every day for the initial few weeks and then weekly until the end of the fermentation period.[17]

After waiting patiently for three long months, he took the mash out and pressed it to drain out the fluid, which was the soy sauce, and the best grade thereof. He heated the sauce at 65°C to kill off any bacteria or mold in the sauce, a process known as pasteurization. To his joy, the first batch was highly successful. The sauce had a pleasing aroma and a marvelous flavor. The brothers tested it in their own cooking and were delighted with their most tasty, appetizing dishes.

He made two more batches, again following the recipe carefully. The results were just as good. He bottled the sauce and sold it in their shop. To their surprise, people returned for more, and all the bottles were sold out within a few days.

When Qiyuan had gained confidence in sauce making, the brothers began to look for a bigger place for sauce production. They rented a house with a larger backyard to place twenty 50-gallon earthenware vessels for fermentation, a kitchen large enough to cook large quantities of beans, and an area adequate to store the finished products.

Initially, they sold the sauce in their own shop. Later, because of heightened demand, the product was distributed to other retail shops for sale. Encouraged by the success, Qiyuan began to experiment making other bean sauces and adding different ingredients. Being a methodical person, he made careful notes on the conditions of each experiment and the result. Not all batches produced good results, but his notes allowed him to identify the mistakes and learned from them. Based on the results of his experiments, Qiyuan began to manufacture different types of bean sauces and pastes. They named their new shop Junhechang Sauce Garden (均和昌醬園). Its business flourished.[18]

By then, the Chen brothers owned a grocery store, a watch and clock repair shop, and a sauce production and retail business. There was no doubt that Qiyuan had demonstrated his ability to take up new challenges. His intelligence and his methodical approach in conducting experiments in a very practical setting—in this instance, making tasty sauces as though in a science laboratory—served him well.

The French Impact

In 1859, about five years after their arrival in Cholon, Saigon and Cholon fell to the French. Vietnamese society was transformed dramatically by the imposition of French rule.

Even though Europeans, mostly missionaries and merchants, first came to Vietnam as early as the sixteenth century, they had little impact on Vietnam. France became more deeply involved only when Nguyen Anh, a Vietnamese lord, sent a delegation to the French court requesting assistance from Louis XVI. The French helped Nguyen establish the Nguyen Dynasty by defeating his rival, the Trinhs, and abolishing the Tay Son Dynasty. The leadership of the new dynasty, however, was consistently weakened by floods, smallpox epidemics, tribal risings, and revolts in the 1840s and 1850s.

Using the persecution of Christian missionaries by the Vietnamese government as an excuse, French forces attacked Vietnam in 1857. Saigon and Cholon were seized in early 1859. In 1862, Emperor Tu, the fourth emperor of Nguyen Dynasty, signed a treaty that ceded the three provinces in southeastern Vietnam to France. (The French referred to this part of Vietnam as Cochinchina). By 1883, all of Vietnam fell under French control. In 1885, despite China's intervention as the suzerain state of Vietnam, France became the protector of Vietnam. In 1887, Cambodia, which became a protectorate of France in 1863, was integrated into French Indochina along with other French colonies and protectorates in Vietnam. Laos also became a protectorate of France in 1893. The whole region, known as the Indochinese Union, consisted of three modern-day countries: Vietnam, Cambodia, and Laos.[19]

The French imposed a heavy poll-tax on Chinese residents initially, but later the tax was broadened to cover all alien Asians in Vietnam.[20] The French, however, encouraged the Chinese in Vietnam to develop roads, railway systems, mining, and industry. This resulted in more Chinese immigrating to that region, and they soon became involved in rice trade and rice milling, eventually establishing a rice monopoly in Vietnam. The Chinese also had a significant presence in sugar refining, coconut and peanut oil production, lumber industry, and shipbuilding.[21]

The increase in immigration, industry, and trade in the region under French colonial administration served to benefit merchants, such as the Chen brothers, who were present in the right place at the right time.

The Fourth Enterprise: Black Gambiered Silk (黑膠綢, Black Jiao Chou) and Cereal Grain Trade

By the time the French took over the administration of Cholon, the Chen brothers were already quite wealthy. They could return to their native village in triumph and retire to enjoy a leisurely life. But the political situation at home had failed to improve. In South Vietnam, the French administration seemed to be providing stability and it encouraged industry and trade. Business opportunities seemed endless. It appeared to be more reasonable and desirable to remain in Vietnam while they were still young.

Qiyuan returned to his native village to visit his family every three years according to customs, but each time he did something more. During these visits, he always had another agenda: to expand their business. Since their arrival in Vietnam, the Chen brothers had been observing and studying the local market, the customs, the food and clothing of the local people. Having not had a great deal of money initially, they adhered to investing in businesses that required a small capital. After six years, the brothers finally had saved enough to go into a more lucrative business which would require a larger capital.

The Vietnamese were fond of black gambiered silk or black Jiao Chou (黑膠綢), which was the first choice of the wealthy for their summer clothing. The material is supple, smooth, waterproof, easy to wash and dry, and durable. The fabric is air permeable, providing coolness and comfort in the summer, and never creasing even under constant pressure. The material is pure natural silk which has undergone an old-fashioned and complicated manufacturing process that has a history of at least 500 years. The dyeing and finishing process, which takes six months, has 14 steps, including yam juicing, soaking, basking, and painting with river mud. The garments made from it rustle delightfully with movement.[22] The Vietnamese preferred black gambiered silk than other colors. Although silk was and is produced in Vietnam, gambiered silk had to be imported from Guangdong because of the complicated, labor-intensive manufacturing process.

Cereal grains, such as soybeans, red beans, green beans, peanuts, and sesame seeds, were consumed by the Chinese but were not grown in Vietnam, even though rice was harvested there in abundance. Qiyuan's task was to find supply sources of these commodities in Guangzhou, the capital of the Guangdong Province, and import the merchandise into Vietnam.[23]

When they returned to Cholon, each brother spearheaded a new business venture according to his natural inclination and talents, and they complemented each other nicely. Qishu with his natural flair for business, friendly and good-natured, took up the retail side of gambiered silk and cereal grains. Soon, more shops were added under their ownership. In addition to the earlier ones (Junhejian Grocery Store, Chenje Watches and Clocks Repair Expert, and Junhechang Sauce Garden), other stores were established to sell rice and imported goods: Yichangyin Silk Store (怡昌蔭號紗綢), Shengqixiang Rice Store (盛其祥谷米行), Yuchang (裕昌), and Tokyo Zhuang (東京莊).[24] Qiyuan, who was more reserved and much more interested in research and investigative work and always enthusiastic in taking up new challenges, began to explore into yet another lucrative business: a pawn shop.

The Fifth Business: Pawn Shop

Another ambitious plan had been brewing in Qiyuan's head for a while. He believed that one could only become more affluent by getting into the "money" business, and this included running a pawn shop. Since ancient times, people around the world have used pawn shops to get money out of their assets quickly. Pawn brokers offered loans to people who used their personal or business property as collateral. These items were (and still are) held by pawn brokers for a contractual period of time during which the owner of the item could repay the secured loan, plus interest, to redeem their items. If the owner was unable to repay the loan to buy them back, the broker had the right to sell the item. Pawn shops emerged in China as early as the Western Han Dynasty in 206 BCE. They were initially established, owned, and operated by Buddhist monasteries. Only later did they become more widely seen in mainstream society.[25]

Qiyuan's task during his third trip home was to learn as much as possible about the pawn shop business. Because he came from a rural family, which seldom had enough for luxuries, he had no idea of the value of old coins, jewelry, paintings, calligraphies, antiques, and other valuable items that people might bring to pawn shops. He found one suitable individual as an appraiser to manage the business and offered him very good terms, including a share of the business—a very smart move, because instead of being just an employee, the person would actually own a portion of the business, and doubtless would work extra hard to ensure the business would prosper. At the same time, to educate himself, Qiyuan collected and read many books that would help him to evaluate various valuables.

Cholon had no pawn shop at that time. The regulations governing pawn shops were strict because in those days, a pawn broker's business was considered charitable. Each city could only have one pawn shop and the owner had to be credible, honest, reliable, and possess reasonably sizable personal assets. The Chen brothers had been in Cholon for 10 years. They owned several shops. It was said that at one time, the shops owned by the Chen brothers occupied half of Canton Street (Figure 3.4). They had already established a very good reputation for honesty in their business transactions and for providing good quality service. A licence to set up the pawn shop business was granted to them upon application without any difficulty.[26]

Figure 3.4. Canton Street, Cholon in 1868. One of shops on the left side bears the name Junhe Oil and Sugar (均和油糖) Junhe was the name of a number of shops owned by the Chen Brothers (Source: "Indochina in Zigzags, "Historic Vietnam by Pierre Billotey, 1928. http://www. Historicvietnam.com /indochina-in-zigzags)

A pawn shop is not an ordinary shop. It needs to be located in a safe and secure environment, yet central and convenient for easy access. It requires more space for staff to live in and for storage of pawned items. It took time for Qiyuan to find such a property that had two stories. The upper floor had two rooms: one for storage and the other to serve as a bedroom for the staff. The arrangement for the ground floor was typical of any pawn shop with an overbearing, high counter, higher than the eye level of the

80

customer. Iron bars, similar to those of a prison cell, rose from the countertop to the ceiling, completely separating the customer from the staff inside to provide security.

Once the suitable property was found, they sent word to the person they had hired in Jiancun to come and manage the business. His main duties were to evaluate the item brought by the customer, assess the condition and marketability of the item, determine the value, the loan, and to be responsible for accounting. Two of the most trustworthy staff from their other shops were transferred to the pawn shop to help with the business. In Vietnam, it was customary for the local people to buy jewelry of gold, precious stones, or diamonds for adornment during good times, and in times of need, to take out a loan from a pawn shop using these valuables as collaterals. The customer was usually given one to five years to reclaim his or her item. The appraiser's role was crucial as the value of the item and the interest paid by the customer determined whether the pawn shop would be profitable or not. As a rule, pawn shops offered lower prices than market value to their customers.

Qiyuan established a number of guidelines for running the pawn shop: 1) honesty is their policy, and all customers are to be treated equally, including women and children; 2) each staff member should be vigilant on his job and safety comes first; 3) the price offered to the customer should be fair; and 4) the owners of the pawn shop should prefer to earn less rather than letting the customers lose a lot of money.[27]

On the opening day of Yifeng Pawn Shop (怡豐餉當), the brothers invited local officials and well-known public figures to the opening ceremony. Lion dances, fireworks and a band of musicians added much to the fanfare of the occasion. Because of their mission statement that "honesty comes first", they had the trust of the local people. Their business thrived. The pawn shop proved to be the most profitable venture of all their businesses in Vietnam, and increasing their wealth considerably.

A Patriot and Philanthropist In the Making

By this time, the Chen brothers had become quite well-off. If they continued to develop their business, they and their descendants would never experience hunger again. But Qiyuan had been constantly bothered by the poverty in their native village. Most of the families in Jiancun were able to feed themselves in good times, but during natural disasters, such as drought and famine, they had to struggle hard to survive. Some desperate parents, unable to feed their children, had to sell their daughters as *mui-tsai* (妹仔). These were young girls sold to wealthy households to become servant-maids for life. They were often maltreated by their owners; some might in turn be sold by their owners into prostitution.

Now that he had acquired significant wealth, what could he do to help people in his native village? Giving them money in times of disaster could only solve the immediate hardship but not the continual poverty. How could he improve the livelihood of the villagers at home and increase the wealth of the region? The answers to Qiyuan's questions would become apparent as the events unfold in the subsequent paragraphs and chapters.

In Qiyuan's ancestral village, sericulture had been a way of life, adding to family income since ancient times. When Qiyuan returned to look for sources of gambiered silk in Guangdong for export to Vietnam, he discovered that it was not easy to find good quality silk. The hand-reeled silk produced in the villages by the traditional method lacked uniformity in smoothness, was uneven in thickness, and had impurities. On the other hand, silk from Vietnam was smooth, uniform in thickness and in color, with a soft, desirable luster. Upon further inquiry, he learned that the silk from Vietnam was reeled by machines.[28] At home, his mother, sisters, and sisters-in-law were using hand-reeled machines, and he had repaired them from time to time in the past. These inefficient machines required the use of both hands to manipulate the cocoons and the silk threads and at the same time to move the reel. The movement was intermittent and uneven. It was not the quality of cocoons but the backward production tools and the reeling method that made Chinese hand-reeled raw silk lose ground in global competition.

Qiyuan figured that the humiliating defeats of the Qing government by foreign powers had a great deal to do with China's lack of technological advances and failure to become as industrialized as the West. He believed, and rightly so, that if he could improve the silk reeling technology, he would be able to produce high quality silk for export and bring prosperity to his native village and the region. Gradually a plan emerged.

Modern Silk Reeling Technology

Very shortly after taking control of Saigon and Cholon in 1859, the French began to install a number of silk filatures powered by steam engines to increase the supply of raw silk to their home country. The epidemic of pebrine disease in 1854 killed 75% of the silkworm culture in Europe and drastically reduced the amount of raw silk for their weaving industry. Qiyuan thought he would visit the filatures which were using the modern French silk reeling machines to learn about the new methods and to introduce them to his native village.

The visit to the silk filatures opened Qiyuan's eyes to the tremendous power of modern technology. The filature was large with several hundred silk reeling machines yet powered by only one steam engine. One worker was responsible for one reeling machine, which had 10 basins, and controlled 10 or more silk threads. The hot water for heating the cocoons was delivered from one boiler, and each worker was able to regulate the temperature of the water in the basins he or she was responsible for. In fact, one worker in the filature was capable of doing the work of 8 to 10 workers who were using hand-reeled machines.[29] The filature produced silk of superior quality, even and smooth with a pleasing sheen, fetching 40% or higher in price than hand-reeled silk.

The visit produced such a profound excitement in Qiyuan that he was unable to sleep sleeping that night, thinking all the time how to change hand-reeled machines to steam-powered machines back home. At around that time, Chinese hand-reeled silk was losing ground to global competition.[30] Japan, where superior quality silk was being produced in filatures, increased its export rapidly and would likely overtake China in raw silk export. Qiyuan believed that the use of steam-powered silk reeling machines back home would increase the production of superior quality raw silk for export to foreign countries. If filatures were to be established in the Pearl River Delta Region, the region would prosper. China might be able to maintain its premier place in raw silk export and improve its economy as a result.

The following day he made enquiries about where silk reeling machines could be purchased. Both England and France produced these machines. If the Chen brothers were to establish a silk filature in Vietnam, all they had to do was submit an application to the government for a licence and proceed with the purchase of the machines from France or England. But if the machines were for a filature in Guangzhou, Britain might not permit the machines to be exported to China. The silk reeling machines for a filature, which employed 300 workers, would cost about 20,000 *taels* of silver; installation and instruction for use of the machines would be another 5,000 *taels* of silver. The initial capital of 25,000 *taels* of silver did not cover the cost of construction of the building to house these machines. In addition, there would be fees for hiring foreign technicians to maintain and repair the machines. The capital investment would be high, but not prohibitive, because the brothers could obtain a loan using the pawn shop as collateral.[31]

In the meantime, Qiyuan had written to a company in London that produced the silk reeling machines. Two months later, he received a most disheartening reply. The company would not sell silk reeling machines to filatures in China; the machines were still under patent rights protection and could not be reproduced. An exception could be made if the filature was owned by a British or a French national. But it was their understanding that the Qing government would not allow foreigners or Chinese merchants to establish such factories in China. Before they could sell machines to a filature in China, a permit from the Qing government would be required.

The reply dampened and cooled Qiyuan's enthusiasm. He had not anticipated so much difficulty. Foreign companies would not sell him steam-powered silk reeling machines for a filature in China. If he purchased only one machine, he would not be able to reproduce it because of patent rights protection. If he were to partner with a foreigner to establish a filature in China, the company would sell him the silk reeling machines, but the Qing government would unlikely give permission. Qiyuan had no solution to overcome the seemingly insurmountable obstacles. The likelihood of this venture to materialize seemed very small indeed.[32]

But Qiyuan was not someone to be put off easily by roadblocks. After contemplating for a few days, an idea struck him. Although he could not buy the machines nor could duplicate them because of patent rights, and no foreigner would teach him the technology, no one could stop him from learning the technology himself. Didn't he learn how to fix clocks and watches by watching surreptitiously without being taught?

With introductions from friends, he began the first of a series of visits to French silk filatures. Warmly received by the manager of the first filature, who thought Qiyuan was a potential customer for raw silk, he gave Qiyuan a tour of the factory. During the tour, the manager explained to Qiyuan the whole process of silk reeling and how the machines worked. Qiyuan poured out a list of questions. At the end of the tour, Qiyuan discovered that there were no mysteries to production of quality silk in the filature; the only difference was that machines did most of the work for the workers. The principle of the silk reeling process remained unchanged.

The friendly manager told Qiyuan that while the silk reeling machines originally had come from China to the West, several new technological advances had been added that were responsible for the superior quality of filature-reeled silk: 1) the adoption of a rigid axle and cogwheel to transmit the power to move and stabilize the reel, replacing a driving belt in the hand-reeled machine; 2) the addition of an extra twisting mechanism (Chambon style in France and Tavelle in Italy)[33] to cross silk threads which greatly enhanced the cohesion, evenness and uniformity of the silk—features that are absolutely essential for high quality raw silk; 3) the use of a centralized steam boiler that provides continuous and even heating of water in the basins for "cooking" cocoons and removal of the fire away from the water basins to eliminate the pollution of silk threads by soot;[34] and 4) the mechanization using steam-powered engines, which came last.

Entrepreneurs in East Asia generally adopted some, but not all four technological improvements. Most traditional silk reelers incorporated the first two features of European reeling technology (cogwheels and crossing systems) into their household-based system. The adoption of the third and the fourth technical innovations required the use of a much larger, centralized location: a silk factory.[35]

After the first visit, Qiyuan formulated some idea as to what could be made in China and what would need to be purchased if he were to proceed with his plan of introducing a modern silk factory in China. To do this, he would require a centralized production system and a steam engine had to be purchased. How the steam engine transferred energy to move the machines was something he had to study in further detail. The reeling machines and the delivery system of hot and cold water separately were simple enough to be made in China.

He was determined to learn the modern silk reeling technology and transfer it to his native land. This was a very courageous decision, as most ordinary Chinese at that time were either illiterate or had received only primary village education. It was hard to imagine how such an individual without any background in physics and mathematics would be able to learn the steam engine technology. Among the employees in the Chen brothers' enterprises, there were a few who had gone through the new primary education curriculum and were more suitable to receive further training. After approaching them one by one, none wished to embark on a project that would take five to six years of learning without any guarantee whether he would succeed or whether the filature project would go ahead after those years. Then Qiyuan thought of learning it himself. Would he be able to learn the techniques necessary for the project at the age of 30? What would happen to the business that he and his brother had built up if he were to go ahead? [36]

Qiyuan reflected on his own experience in Vietnam over the past 10 years. When he first came to Vietnam, he knew very little about business. But, step by step he learned how to run a grocery store, repair watches and clocks, manufacture sauces, handle import-export business, and even run a pawn shop. Each set of skills and knowledge had been acquired and improved further with time. His confidence in his own abilities returned after this contemplation. Where there is a will, there is a way.

At the age of 30 he had passed the usual age of schooling and should have been well-established in life, which he was. To return to study science and technology without a background in mathematics and physics would be a long-drawn, trying process. The whole course would have to be self-taught because no school would provide him with all the specific knowledge required. He would have to give up most of the responsibilities in the business and halt expanding it further for the next five to six years. Would Qishu, his brother, agree to this seemingly unprofitable or even money-losing venture for five to six years?

An Unusual Path

When Qiyuan approached his brother with this unusual and surprising plan, Qishu was moved by his enthusiasm and patriotism and wisely left his brother to make the decision. If Qiyuan were to go ahead with the project, Qishu would support him by taking over most of the responsibilities in running the business. But Qishu also cautioned that the project would be long and difficult; if it failed, Qiyuan would have missed the opportunities in business during the best years of his life.[37]

After a great deal of consideration, Qiyuan came to the conclusion that he would take up the new challenge for the betterment of the lives of people in his native village and his country, a decision that did not come easily because of the sacrifice involved. Having made up his mind how was he to proceed?

During the tour of the first filature, he met Mr. Lee, a compatriot from Taishan (台山), who was an experienced mechanic responsible for maintenance work in the filature. Mr. Lee was around 40 years old and had been with the filature since its inception. He could not understand why a well-heeled man like Qiyuan would give up his chances of earning much more money in the next five to six years and instead, would go back to study the basics of silk machinery;

but he admired Qiyuan's lofty goal. Extremely sympathetic to Qiyuan's bold and unselfish plan, Mr. Lee worked out the curriculum for Qiyuan. Qiyuan would need to study mathematics, physics, mechanics, the steam engine, and basic drafting.[38]

There were so many new things to learn. Qiyuan started to collect as many books as possible from Cholon, Saigon, and Guangzhou on the topics he would have to study. He immersed himself in his pile of books and spent many days and sleepless nights trying to understand the different topics. When he encountered problems, he would visit Lee, who became indispensable to Qiyuan as a friend and teacher in the ensuing years. Once the theories were out of the way, Qiyuan began to learn the application of theories to practice.

Two different kinds of machines were crucial to the function of a modern filature: the silk reeling machines and the steam engine that powered them. Qiyuan believed that the silk reeling machines could be built in China, but a blueprint of the machine would be required. He had also decided that although no foreign company would sell him a steam engine and no company in China would be able to build one, he would buy a boiler from an old ship to generate steam and learn how to use the energy from steam to drive the machines. It was not difficult to gain invitations to visit the filatures in Vietnam because of his reputation, wealth, and his potential to be a customer for raw silk.

With his excellent eyesight and his ability to see clearly from a distance, no one could have guessed that he was making copies of different parts of the machine in his head. After returning home from each visit, he would immediately make drawings of the parts of the machine on paper. He measured the size of the different parts by comparing them with his fingers or his arm. He would always ask Lee to check the accuracy of his drawings.

He visited filatures not only in Cholon and Saigon, but also those in Hanoi and Bangkok.[39] After making drawings of the silk reeling machine, he made drawings of the filature indicating how and where the machines were organized and connected. He noted that there were areas or rooms in the filature for other important activities: cocoon storage, cocoon drying, cocoon sorting, and cocoon cooking.[40] Next, he learned about the logistics in the filature, the number of employees and their job descriptions. Lastly, he studied the management and the financial aspects of the filature.

Qiyuan made many drawings over the years. These drawings formed the basis of the machines that would be made for his filature. No one in the Vietnamese filatures that he had visited suspected that he was "stealing" their technology. The European managers did not believe that the Chinese would be able to make such machines, based on the misconception that they were poorly educated and knew nothing about science and technology.[41]

Voyage Home

At the end of the six years of study and hard work, Qiyuan felt that he had learned everything about silk filatures, how they worked, and how to run them. It was time to return home and put his six years' learning into practice. He left Vietnam in 1872 with a thankful heart, bringing with him a chest full of drawings, all the new knowledge that he had acquired during the past 18 years and, of course, considerable wealth.

This time, Qiyuan travelled from Saigon to Hong Kong on a steamship. In addition to carrying cargo, the ship had compartments for passengers. Traveling with him were two men, Ah Fu (阿福) and Ah Liang (阿良), who he had recruited from Xiqiao to manage his shops in Cholon. These two individuals had also visited filatures and learned about silk reeling in Vietnam, and they would form the nucleus of his team to start the filature back home. Qiyuan also purchased an old ship boiler to be incorporated into a steam engine. It was taken apart and shipped home.[42]

On this occasion, Qiyuan must have been in a very optimistic mood as he showed off in public his superb vision for the first time. Qiyuan told his companions in the presence of the Captain of the boat, "Look! There is a huge steamship coming toward us." When the Captain, an Englishman who understood some Cantonese, heard this, he strained his eyes to look for the steamship and was unable to detect anything amidst the vast ocean. He picked up his telescope and saw nothing. Qiyuan said, "Wait for five minutes, and look again with your telescope." Five minutes later, the Captain did as he was told and there was the steamship cruising towards them. The Captain was dumbfounded. He asked Qiyuan for his name and recorded the event. He even published it in an

English newspaper in Hong Kong, introducing Qiyuan as someone with extraordinary power.[43]

It took Qiyuan and his companions only three to four days to reach Hong Kong. From there, they travelled for another two days to reach Jiancun, Xiqiao.

For most of the Chinese emigrants who had been away from home for almost twenty years, it would be time to enjoy a good life in retirement. For Qiyuan, however, it was another story. It was the beginning of a completely different journey, a new career as a sophisticated entrepreneur and a silk filature specialist to realize his dream of improving the economy of his native village and of the Pearl River Delta Region.

Chapter 4: Jichanglong (繼昌隆) —The First Chinese Silk Filature in South China

Qiyuan saw the gradual recovery of Guangdong's economy in the late 1860s after years of war and instability from the Taiping Rebellion. The Qing government and the Mandarins finally realized the backwardness and weakness of China compared to the Western countries. They began the Self-Strengthening Movement in order to improve the military might of their own country, and at the same time, they also began to carry out some reforms in trade and industry.

Qiyuan returned from Vietnam in 1872—perfect timing to enter into the silk business when both the demand and the price of raw silk had risen sharply. A great deal of obstacles still lay ahead before he could set up a filature. He needed to find a suitable place to build it. It was a blessing that he had learned so much about the silk reeling process and the machines in the filature, because the lack of infrastructure to build the modern machines necessitated considerable modifications. It would be a challenge to ensure his version of the silk reeling machines could produce quality reeled silk. This was indeed a very bold experiment to introduce modern industry to a primitive ancient country such as China because of the socio-economic consequences.

Where to establish the first silk filature in South China?

During his last triennial visit to his native village from Annam, Qiyuan had gathered information on various aspects of the silk industry in different places in Guangdong to help him to decide where to establish his silk filature. When he returned from Annam in 1872, he toured Shanghai and the Yangtze River Delta area, the famous silk-producing region, to learn more from the experiences of other places.[1]

The idea of establishing a silk filature in China was not new in 1872. As early as 1859, Jardine, Matheson & Co, a powerful British trading firm, established the first silk filature using European technology in Shanghai, a treaty port. Construction began in 1860. To construct a modern-style factory with 100 machines driven by steam power proved to be trouble-ridden and protracted in Shanghai, which then had virtually no industry. In 1863, the Ewo Silk Filature (怡和絲廠) was finally open, but John Major, the operator of the filature, had considerable problems securing a stable workforce with sufficient skill and discipline. He recruited four French women, highly skilled in silk reeling, to train the local workforce. After a stable workforce was established, he was still unable to obtain a reliable supply of cocoons. Ewo Silk Filature was established in Shanghai based on the assumption that its hinterland, the lower Yangtze Delta, would provide the raw material for silk reeling. This assumption proved fatal because Shanghai was 100 miles away from the sericulture region, outside the treaty port area where direct foreign investment was not allowed. Moreover, Ewo was faced with high transportation cost and lack of drying facilities in the rural area where the cocoons were produced. To make matters worse, there was fierce local resistance from the organized silk handicraft and commercial guilds, fearing the loss of cocoon supply to the filature. Ewo encountered deficits every year since its opening, and closed its doors in 1869 when Major died.[2]

From this, Qiyuan learned several important lessons: 1) reeling factories should be located near cocoon-producing regions because it takes six pounds of fresh cocoons to produce one pound of silk, thus transporting finished raw silk would be far cheaper than shipping fresh cocoons; 2) a stable, well-trained workforce was essential; 3) be prepared for resistance from organized guilds because of loss of silk market and loss of supply of fresh cocoons; and 4) support from the local community was vital for success.

He had three possibilities in mind for his filature's location: Guangzhou, Shunde, and his native village, Jiancun. The Chinese government prohibited private involvement in cotton spinning in 1872 because the government itself had been planning a mechanized spinning plant. Qiyuan excluded Guangzhou, the capital of Guangdong Province, where establishing a filature would certainly attract the attention of local officials. Shunde was an ideal place because of its geography, a gateway to Guangzhou and its proximity to Hong Kong and Macau. Its efficient waterway network provided transportation from its hinterland covered with mulberry dike-fish ponds.[3] Qiyuan was tempted to establish his first filature in Shunde, but there he lacked the support of the local community.

He opted instead for his native village Jiancun for several reasons, one of which was that it had an efficient waterway for transport. He wanted to benefit his native village with this project, he knew people in his own village, and he could do considerable public relations and promotional works within the local community. Jiancun, being a village, would less likely come to the attention of the authorities. Moreover, he needed a stable workforce and this could come from his native village as well as villages nearby. As he would be hiring mostly women, who could work during the day and return home in the evening, there was no need to provide them with accommodation. The waste products such as the dead silkworms and their excreta could be used to feed the fish on the fish farm nearby and further benefit the local community.[4]

He purchased an empty lot next to his ancestral home for the filature.[5] A stream on the east side of the property provided the necessary water for the use of the filature and a perfect means for transporting raw materials such as cocoons, coal, and firewood. One could readily make a return boat trip to neighboring Shunde, Guangzhou, and Foshan within a day.

Financing the Venture

Qiyuan had previously obtained information on the capital necessary for the filature if he were to purchase all the machinery from the West for a filature employing 300 workers (about 25,000 *taels* of silver), but now that he was making the machines locally, the project would cost less. He decided that the silk filature would be financed by the Chen family. He had already spent 1,000 *taels* of silver to purchase an old boiler. He transferred from Annam to Jiancun another 7,000 *taels* of silver, of which 3,000 *taels* accounted for operating expenses when the filature opened. In total, he had earmarked 10,000 *taels* for this venture.[6] It was to be a family business—the first factory built in South China solely financed by Chinese without aid from any other source.

Building the Silk Reeling Machines

When Qiyuan returned to his native village from Annam in the 1870s, China had little industry and very little experience in the manufacturing or maintenance of machinery. In Jiancun, he found no machine shop nor a skilled technician who could help him to do such a job.[7]

Qiyuan took all the blueprints with him to Guangzhou and looked for machinery shops. By chance he came across one machinery shop, Chen Liantai Company (陳聯泰號) in Xindoulan Sheng Jie, Shisanhang (新豆欄上街,十三行), owned by Chen Danpu (陳淡浦) and his two sons, Lianchuan and Taochuan (濂川, 桃川). A native of Xiqiao, Nanhai, Chen Danpu started his business making sewing machines. Later, he turned to machine repair. Danpu also ran an installation of engines and repair service for steamships and learned the technology related to the steam engine.[8] The two Chens, with the same family name and from the same county, became great friends and partners in business.

99

Qiyuan would be responsible for designing the machines and Danpu would be responsible for making and installing them.[9]

After assessing what was available and feasible locally, Qiyuan knew that he had to modify the Western silk reeling machine for local production. He could only make use of the most crucial two out of the four new technologies to improve the quality of raw silk: 1) the use of the French Chambon system for twisting and crossing the silk threads; and 2) the use of a centralized steam boiler to ensure continuous, even heating of water in the basins to soften the sericin and facilitate the unwinding of filaments without breaks. The installation of a steam boiler would also eliminate the use of coal fire near the basins and soot pollution of the silk threads. He added a Chinese touch to the silk reeling process—to use the all-purpose Chinese chopsticks to pick out fibers from cocoons in the boiling basins.[10]

It was not possible at that time for Danpu to build the parts of the steam engine that could transfer steam energy to drive a large number of reeling machines in the factory. He did not have adequate facilities then, but these could come later. In the meantime, the power to drive the machines could be supplied by people using foot treadles; after all, there was no shortage of cheap manual labor in China.

Once the building of the factory had been completed, it was turned into carpenter-cum-machinery shop, where the different components of the silk reeling machines were made and assembled. Because of the high cost of steel and metal work, Qiyuan substituted them with wood wherever feasible, for example, the reels and the supporting frame of the workstations would be made of wood (Figure 4.4, 4.5).

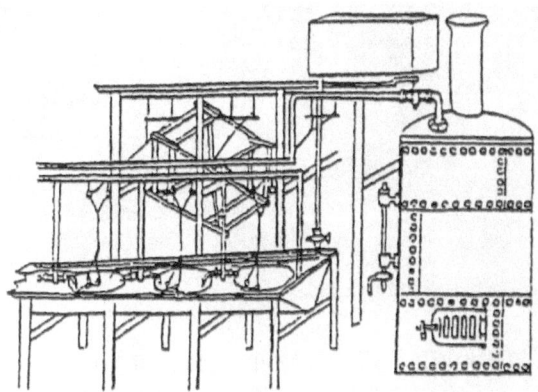

Figure 4.4. Silk reeling machine with steam-heated water delivered to the basins (Source: *Can Sang Pu* [蠶桑譜, *On Sericulture*], Guangxi Normal University Press, 2015), opposite 86)

Chen Danpu provided a team of four technicians to work with the four assistants hired by Qiyuan. Chen Qiyuan's staff also participated in building the reeling machines and they would become maintenance mechanics when the factory began to operate.[11] Chen Danpu was a genius when it came to modification and adaptation of machines for local use. Between the two Chens, the silk reeling machines were built at one-fifth of the cost of those

101

powered by steam engines. Chen Danpu would later become an expert in this area and the main supplier of silk reeling machines in the region.[12]

Figure 4.5. Silk reeling machine with multiple basins displayed in Chen Qiyuan Memorial Hall (photo by May Kaan)

Jichanglong (繼昌隆): The First Chinese Silk Filature in South China

After eight to nine months of cooperative work between the two teams, the filature was able to start operation. Multiple tests had been done to ensure that the filature was functioning properly. Qiyuan hired and trained about 100 female workers and purchased cocoons and fuel. He chose a propitious date for the opening ceremony of the filature, which he named Jichanglong, meaning "continue to prosper." He invited all the gentry and elders in Jiancun and neighboring villages to the opening, which was celebrated with lion dances, firecrackers, and gongs to drive away the evil spirits. Over 400 guests arrived. Never before had Jiancun seen such a huge gathering. In 1873, Jichanglong had the following equipment:

1) A cylindrical steam engine of 1.2 *zhang* high (1 *zhang* [丈] = 10.94 feet), 0.6 *zhang* wide, installed to generate energy for the water pump to bring river water into the factory and to send steam generated from the boiler furnace to the work stations. The engine was also attached to a high smokestack of 3.6 *zhang* equipped with whistles, which sent out signals three times in the mornings.

2) One boiler furnace used to generate steam, 1.5 *zhang* high, 0.7 to 0.8 *zhang* wide; one huge tank for storage of river water.

3) Rows of basin units driven by foot treadles to power silk reeling. Each of the basins, to heat up the cocoons, had two sets of pipes, one for delivering steam and one for cold water. At the bottom of each basin was a metallic plate through which a pipe carrying stream was attached. This arrangement enabled the heat from the steam to be evenly distributed to the basin. If the water temperature in the basin was too high, it could be adjusted by opening the cold-water faucet located in front of each basin.

4) Rows of silk reeling equipment made of wood.

5) Chambers for drying and storing cocoons.[13]

There were 100 basins in Jichanglong when it first opened for operation. Basins and other necessary equipment were continuously being added and installed after its opening. At the end of one year of operation, the number of basins increased to 300, and in later years, it rose to 700.[14]

The silk produced by Jichanglong was superior to home-reeled silk. It was even, uniform in quality, lustrous, more elastic, and clean.[15] It suited foreign weaving machines and was entirely for exports. Jichanglong silk fetched higher prices than the home-reeled silk by about 30 to 40%.[16]

Qiyuan explained why Jichanglong's silk was of good quality. First, the use of steam enabled water temperature of the basin kept constant at around 160° F. This maintained the luster of the silk fiber and also kept the "melting state" of the gummy substance optimal for the unwinding of silk fibers from cocoons. The steam through pipes could reach hundreds of basins simultaneously, thus improving the efficiency. Second, foot-treadle-powered reeling freed both hands of the reelers for reeling and for clearing the floss of the cocoons. Third, the Chambon system (Figure 4.6, Figure 4.7) increased cohesion and elasticity of the silk products. Fourth, cocoons were carefully sorted and graded before reeling. Finally, the rules of choosing the number of cocoons for reeling were strictly adhered to (see below), so that the fineness and coarseness of each silk skein wound met the specifications of the foreign requirement. Two types of fine silk were produced depending on the country to which it was exported: silk of 13/15 denier measure (used 6/7 cocoons) for export to Europe and silk of 14/16 denier (used 8/9 cocoons) for export to the United States.[17]

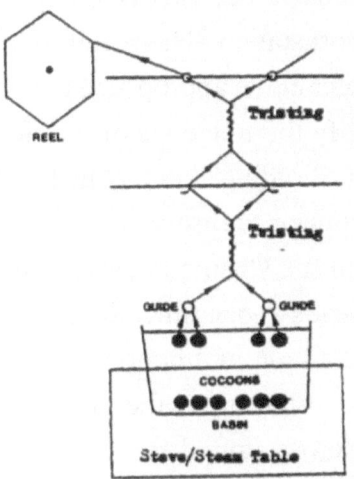

Figure 4.6. French Chambon winding system (Source: Wong, "Proto indust-rialization and the Silk Industry of the Canton Delta, 1662– 1934", 74

Figure 4.7. The basins and the Chambon winding system dispalyed in Chen Qiyuan Memorial Hall (photo by author)

Cocoons, which had been sorted and graded, would be delivered to each workstation. The reeler would place them in the basin with water at the appropriate temperature. Using a chopstick to identify the free ends of the fibers from three to four cocoons and holding them with her left hand, the reeler used her right hand to throw the fibers of the cocoons into the thread. With the Chambon system, the reeler could manage two silk threads at one time. Each of the two threads first passed through a hole in a button and then passed to a hook above. Before going up to the hook, the two threads were first twisted to cross around each other, a process called down-twisting. The device for twisting consisted of an arrangement of gears and wheels which gave 200 twists when its handle was turned once. After the threads passed over the hooks, they were twisted again, called up-twisting, and passed to the reel to be wound into skeins. During this process, the reeler had to be very careful to watch the cocoons that were unwinding and to maintain the same number of cocoons to a thread all the time.[18] Defects of raw silk mostly came from an improper method of reeling or from the reeler's carelessness.[19]

Since steam was not used as the power source to drive the reels, Jichanglong was actually a centralized handicraft workshop, where women workers gathered together using foot treadles to power the reeling machines and steam was used only to produce even heating of the cocoons to improve the quality of raw silk.[20]

Figure 4.8. Model of steam-pwered silk reeling machine displayed in Chen Qiyuan Memorial Hall (photo by May Kaan)

Management at Jichanglong

Chen Qiyuan put in place a number of innovations in management. He tapped into the female labor force and placed women in a centralized location where men also worked. This was unheard of in China with the exception of Ewo Filature in Shanghai, which had closed its doors in 1869.

In addition to the 100 female silk reelers of Jichanglong when it first opened, Qiyuan had another 30 people on staff. He acted as manager and was assisted by Ah Fu and Ah Liang, the two individuals who he had brought with him to and from Annam. Additionally, he hired an accountant who also acted as the sales manager. There were other staff for various duties such as for drying the cocoons and for packaging the reeled silk into bags which each contained 80 *catties* of reeled silk. Plus, he hired the inspectors, the mechanic and his assistants for maintenance of the machines, and employees for miscellaneous duties. The salary for various people was between 6 to 8 *taels* of silver per month.[20] Technicians and maintenance staff with special skills were paid more. Over time, Jichanglong expanded to include at one time up to 800 workers.

To run a factory with several hundred people was new in China, where factories were almost non-existent. He realized that it was important to have some rules and regulations for workers to follow and established a system of bonuses and fines to encourage good practices and discourage undesirable ones.[21]

The silk reelers were all female and were paid by the amount of reeled silk they produced per day. In general, a skilled reeler could produce around three *taels* of reeled silk each day and received payment of 0.12 to 0.15 *taels* of silver. The monthly salary was usually around 3.76 to 4.5 *taels* of silver, paid bi-monthly. If there was no absence from work and the amount of reeled silk produced had been steady, a reeler would receive a bonus of three days' salary each month. In addition, she would be eligible for annual and seasonal bonuses.[22] As a result, there were seldom any vacant positions in Jichanglong.

On the other hand, a penalty was imposed on those who did not turn up for work, who arrived late or left early, or who produced poor quality work. The penalty would be deducted from the salary of the offender.

Since the pay was dependent on the amount of reeled silk, some reelers tried to increase the weight of reeled silk by adding more filaments from more cocoons to each silk thread (five or six instead of three or four cocoons). This would make the reeled silk thicker and uneven. To discourage this practice, inspectors were hired to carry out inspections both in the open and discreetly. There were holes in the mezzanine floor of the building where the inspectors could obtain a bird's eye view of the reelers to detect this malpractice. When the reeler was caught the first time, she would be warned and fined one day's salary. When caught the second time for the same offence, in addition to a fine of one day's pay, one month's bonus would be withdrawn. The third offence would lead to permanent dismissal with no chance of being hired again. To prevent theft of silk from the filature by reelers, two female supervisors would carry out an inspection at the end of the day when the reelers left the filature for their homes. Offenders would be punished in the same way as above.[23]

Daily Routine Operation

Every morning, Jichanglong sounded its whistle three times. The first loud, shrill whistle was to wake up the workers in the village, the second signaled them to go work, and the third for the filature to close its door when work began. Those who arrived late would not be admitted for the day and would be counted as absent from work.[24] In those days, keeping time was not considered essential in rural communities in China. Very few had clocks at home. In the beginning, the workers were not used to this strict routine, but gradually they became accustomed to it.[25]

The working day started at 7 a.m. and ended at 5 p.m. with one hour of rest for lunch from noon to 1 p.m.[26] Those who lived some distance away would bring their uncooked lunch to work as the filature hired some elderly women to cook their lunches for them. One woman would cook lunch for about 10 workers. These elderly women all received a rice card to obtain 20 *catties* of free rice each month from Qiyuan's rice shop in the village, and they also received some payment for their service as cooks in the filature. After lunch, the workers had about 20 to 30 minutes of rest before starting their afternoon work. The free cooking was considered a benefit provided by the filature.

At the end of the day, the reeler would remove the reeled silk from the reel and cover it with an oiled cloth. The reeled silk would be registered, collected, weighed, and placed in a special room to keep it dry. A day's work usually amounted to about 2 to 3 *taels* of raw silk. The reeled silk would be ready for packaging for export.[27]

Shrewd Business Strategies

Unlike Ewo, Jichanglong made a profit during the first year of its operation.[28] Years of conducting business in Annam had prepared Qiyuan to be very astute, always anticipating and responding to possible problems. To keep the filature going, there had to be an adequate supply of cocoons. At that time, the rural households still had hand-operated reeling machines and their own supply of cocoons. The peasants usually processed the raw material themselves and few would sell the cocoons in the markets. To secure cocoon supply, Qiyuan sent out agents to purchase cocoons not only from the surrounding town of Xiqiao, but also from neighboring counties such as Shunde, Zongshan (中山), and Dongguan. To preserve the quality of the cocoons, he obtained permission from local temples to use their spacious compounds to dry the fresh cocoons before transporting them to his filature.[29]

Three months into the operation of Jichanglong, two cocoon markets were set up at Guanshan (官山), a large market town in Xiqiao. Two others were added later. Qiyuan immediately invested money into these cocoon markets. As an entrepreneur, Chen Qiyuan applied economic incentives to ensure a good supply of cocoons for his filature. He offered a high price for cocoons, so that the peasants would switch over from home silk reeling to cocoon production. He generously lent peasants money with low interest, earmarked for cocoon production.[30] These strategies proved to be fruitful.

Jichanglong produced reeled silk solely for export. Qiyuan believed strongly that China should produce superior quality silk in large quantities for export, so that foreign money would return to China to offset the funds being constantly drained away by payment of huge indemnity obligations and debts becauset of the opium wars. Increasing export to foreign countries was one of the ways to revitalize the economy of the village, the Pearl River Delta, and the country.

In those days, Chinese silk was exported to foreign countries by foreign firms. Sales agents and managers of silk commission houses (*sizhuang*, 絲莊) representing the filatures, sold raw silk to the foreign export firms. There were about 20 such commission houses in Guangzhou in 1925. Silk was sent by boats from filatures such as Jichanglong and others to the commission house for storage and sale. Each day an agent from the commission house visited the foreign export firms. He would be paid a fixed commission of 0.8% of sales or a fixed salary. Their counterparts at the foreign firm, the compradors, were reimbursed with a 0.15% commission, out of which they paid the salaries and wages of men they hired. To bypass the middlemen and to facilitate his overseas sales, Qiyuan set up his own commission house (Changzan Sizhuang, 昌棧絲莊) in Guangzhou, managed by his son, Chen Puxuan (陳蒲軒)[31] Changzan Sizhuang also represented several other filatures in dealings with the foreign exporters. Puxuan could not speak English, but he learned some key phrases. He also hired someone who could speak English to negotiate with the foreign firms.

There was, however, no way that Qiyuan could extend his business to complete the final step in the silk-export trade: to sell Jichanglong silk directly to foreign countries overseas. Export of silk at Guangzhou and Shanghai was entirely controlled by foreign firms after the Second Opium War, some of which were general merchants such as Jardine, Matheson & Co., and other were specialists in silk or branches of European and American silk houses. French,

British, and Italian firms monopolized silk exports. These foreign firms used various means to increase their profit, often by deliberate fault-finding of the product and bargaining for the lowest prices. For example, the foreign firms reserved the right to reject the consignment upon delivery if the goods were found to be unsatisfactory. If the goods were returned, the foreign firm was not responsible for costs or damage incurred during inspection. Payment to the Chinese filature was made only after the goods were on board the ship, and the filature was responsible for the payment of the various export taxes. If the Chinese filature failed to deliver the silk on time, the foreign firm could cancel the contract unilaterally and hold the Chinese merchant for penalty. If the Western house had not issued its notification to deliver, the Chinese concern must wait, even on the specified date of delivery, thereby incurring losses due to additional rent, insurance, and interest payment.[32] Because of the extraterritorial privileges and legal immunities enjoyed by Western companies, it was difficult for the Chinese silk manufacturers to negotiate for better terms with the Westerners.

Qiyuan could not change the semi-colonial status of his own country at that time because it was beyond his control. However, he could help strengthen the economy of his country by using his expertise in producing high quality silk for export.

Criticisms and Opposition

It is inevitable that such a large undertaking, like a factory with 300 and later 800 female workers in a rural area, would lead to social changes in the community. Even before Jichanglong was built, Qiyuan had anticipated opposition and resistance in the village. He met with the elders in the village, the students he taught in the Joy of Farming *si-shu*, his friends, and relatives. He explained patiently to them about the factory that he wanted to build and the economic benefits it might bring to the community. The factory with the new machines was not going to replace manpower. Far from it, the machines would produce good quality silk for export and financially benefit the village. Although machines might eventually replace the work of some people, this would be some time in the future. The older generation was quite skeptical of the use of machines, but young people were keen to see it put in practice.[33]

In addition to improving public relations, he started a number of philanthropic activities, such as establishing meat and grocery shops to provide cheaper food for the villagers, setting up a herbal store to give free medical consultation and herbal medicine to the poor, and founded a free school for children from poor families[34] (see Chapter 6). Despite all his public relations efforts, public service, and philanthropic activities, criticisms of Jichanglong abounded, both from vested interests and conservative, closed-minded locals, even though he had support from some village elders.

The three whistles in the morning were a constant source of complaint. To some they were "ghosts' shrills" and disturbed the peace in the village. The chimneystack, several *zhangs* high, was unsightly, and its black smoke polluted the air. The black smoke from the chimneys, casting dark shadows on their ancestral temple and the nearby cemetery, would bring sinister omens. The most serious concern was the mix of men and women in the workplace, which was against the teaching of Confucius and considered conducive to inappropriate behavior.[35] The possibility of job loss when one steam-powered reeling machine could perform the work of 10 people was constantly brought up. Since the reeled silk was for export to foreigners, the silk reeling machine in the filature was called "ghost-reeling machine." The traditionalists asked why they should discard their age-old, home-built machines, which had served them well for centuries, in favor of the "ghost-machines."[36]

Qiyuan thought his public relations efforts were not thorough enough when he heard all these criticisms. He then sought out an educated group of people including two brothers, both *juren*, who were influential in Xuetang (學堂) village nearby. They were involved at one time with the hand-reeled silk business. Qiyuan had hoped that these two educated brothers might be able to help him to spread the word on the beneficial aspects of mechanized silk reeling, but the pair proved to be the wrong choice. The two brothers practically threw Qiyuan out of their doors, believing that the machines in the filature were "ghost-machines" and should be destroyed. Interestingly, two years later, these two brothers called on Qiyuan, humbly begging for information on how to set up a filature, seeing how much wealth

Jichanglong brought into the community. Qiyuan offered them the same enthusiastic support as he did for anyone interested in his technology. The two brothers subsequently established a filature in Xuetang village, but at the wrong time. Their arrogance and mismanagement, as described in the following chapter, brought disaster to their own filature and those in Nanhai.[37]

Knowledge Sharing

Qiyuan was keen to disseminate his technology. During the first three years of operating Jichanglong, he had over 1,000 visitors, over 300 each year.[38] When he created his own version of the silk reeling machine to produce high quality silk, he could have kept the secret to himself, but he did not. He wanted his invention to benefit as many people as possible. He explained to his visitors patiently about the new technology, and he shared his blueprints readily to anyone who asked for his advice. He even recommended Chen Danpu to anyone who was interested in setting up a filature. Chen Danpu's business grew as a result. Qiyuan believed that the more filatures built, the better, as more silk exported would generate regional and even national prosperity. Advancement in the silk trade would certainly stimulate development of other businesses in the area.

Qiyuan's willingness to share and disseminate his knowledge led to rapid spreading of silk reeling factories in Nanhai and neighboring counties. By 1881, there were 10 filatures in Nanhai and six in Shunde. In Jiancun alone, there were four filatures.[39] The development of filatures inevitably brought along significant social changes in the community, but ultimately created problems.

Chapter 5: The 1881 Silk Weavers' Riot and the Macau Interlude (1882 to 1885)

The success of Jichanglong was a powerful confirmation of Qiyuan's belief in the importance of technology in silk reeling. His undertaking was modelled after the Confucian teaching: "To obtain a good result, one needs good tools (工欲善其事，必先利其器)." Qiyuan's willingness to share his knowledge led to the progressive sprouting of silk filatures not only in Nanhai County, but also neighboring counties, such as Shunde, Xiangshan, and Dongguan

Qiyuan was fully aware of the possible conflicts when modern technology was first introduced to a traditional society accustomed to long-established methods of doing things. He recognized the potential sources of conflict between the weavers, who used hand-reeled silk, and the owners of silk filatures. Both producers of filature silk and domestic hand-reeled silk were competing for cocoons and the supply of which was limited. Filature owners could afford to send agents to purchase cocoon not only from the surrounding villages but also from neighboring counties. In the year when cocoon harvest was poor, there might not be enough cocoons to satisfy both groups, and domestic silk reelers and weavers would be much more adversely affected than the filature owners. The rising price of raw silk due to the growing demand in the global market enabled filature owners, such as Qiyuan, to offer a higher price for cocoons as incentive to encourage the peasantry to switch from home silk reeling to cocoon production.[1] In addition, there was a competition for the workforce. Since the filatures paid a higher salary, most of the women opted to work in silk filatures rather than to work at home to produce hand-reeled silk. The difficulty in obtaining hand-reeled silk from lack of cocoons and the preference for women to work in filatures threatened the livelihood of the silk weavers.[2]

The Silk Weavers' Guild: Jingluntang (錦綸堂)

The hand-reeled silk had been produced largely for domestic use. Before the First Opium War, silk only accounted for a small percentage of total exports from China. Silk reeling and silk weaving were conducted as cottage industries, mostly in rural areas. In urban areas, the largest workshop only had 20 weavers. Silk weavers' guilds, which had immense power over their members, thrived in the late Qing Dynasty in Guangzhou, Foshan, Nanhai, and Panyu. In the 1860s, Nanhai had 30,000 to 40,000 weavers who belonged to Jingluntang, the guild association of silk weavers. In Xiqiao alone, there were some 3,000 to 4,000 weavers.[3] These guilds maintained mutually exclusive territories, had rules and regulations within their trade, collected dues to enforce guild regulations, and provided for the needs of indigent members and their bereaved dependents. The guilds also acted as government tax collectors in exchange for monopolistic rights.[4]

Jinglungtang was the largest silk weavers' guild organization in Guangzhou, and in the counties of Nanhai and Shunde. It was an unruly organization, powerful and militarized. It organized militias that took part in civic duties, such as firefighting and fighting bandits, and planned strikes and protests. The members even participated in fighting against the British forces in Guangzhou during the First Opium War.[5] Some members of this guild also belonged to the Heaven and Earth Society (天地會), which was responsible for the local uprising in support of the Taiping Rebellion.

To avoid any misunderstanding and possible opposition from the silk weavers' guild, Jingluntang, Qiyuan visited it and met with its director shortly after the opening of his filature. Qiyuan carefully explained to the director the nature of his filature and that it aimed at producing good quality raw silk for export only. The director was more concerned with the rumor that a single machine in Jichanglong could do the work of ten hand-reelers, which would result in the inevitable loss of jobs in the villages. Qiyuan explained that the machines in Jichanglong at that time were quite incapable of doing that. The silk reeling process was highly labor intensive. The director of Jingluntang asked more questions to ensure that the silk weavers' interests were not affected by the existence of Jichanglong. Upon seeing that Jichanglong had only about 100 to 200 employees at that time, the director concluded that as long as there was no conflict of interest, he was quite prepared to recognize the coexistence of Jichanglong with the hand-reeled silk industry.[6]

In view of the notorious history of the Jingluntang and its propensity for violence, and despite the reassurance from its director, Qiyuan quietly prepared for a possible confrontation in the future. He formed a small group comprising of his own grown-up sons, male workers from the filature, and willing participants who were on his payroll to protect the filature if needed. He purchased guns and swords and prepared them for a possible violent conflict. Unfortunately his preparation was not in vain.[7]

The apparent peace with Jingluntang did not last long. The growing number of filatures in the region, 10 in the recent three years, heightened the competition for cocoons and the cost to procure hand-reeled silk. Many weavers lost their jobs as they were unable to obtain raw hand-reeled silk. Hunger bred hostility and anger towards the filatures which they thought had destroyed their livelihood.

The Silk Weavers' Riot of 1881[8]

The spring of 1881 had been unusually wet. Heavy rain, sometimes in torrents, fell most of that season. Many areas along the Pearl River in Guangdong and Guangxi suffered from flooding. As mulberry dikes were inundated with water, mulberry leaves failed to grow. Many mulberry trees died. Silkworms do not tolerate wet mulberry leaves, and they also died. In the past, there had been poor harvests due to bad weather conditions. Most of the time, subsequent crops of silkworms could make up the deficit. In Guangdong, silkworms were multivoltine, meaning that they hatched several times, sometimes up to seven or eight times each year. The prolonged rain in the summer months of that year led to a poor harvest of cocoons throughout the year and further aggravated the plight of the hand-reelers and the weavers.[9] Unable to obtain cocoon supply, the reelers stopped working, and the weavers had no raw silk to work with. By fall of that year, their discontent and anger escalated.

On 13 August 1881 (lunar calendar), Jingluntang held its annual feast in the Sifu Temple (師傅廟) in Dagang market (大崗) in Nanhai County. The director of Jingluntang and the Temple host had planned to use this opportunity, when most weavers gathered together, to organize a force to destroy the filatures and their machines. They decided to target first Yuhouchang (裕厚昌), the filature of the Chen brothers, Chen Zhiqu (陳植榘), and Chen Zhishu (陳植恕), who were both jurens. The brothers had infuriated the guild officials by prohibiting the workers in their filature to pay dues to the guild and had also informed the county magistrate of the presence of members of the Heaven and Earth Society in the guild. Yuhouchang, which was located in Xuetang village, close to the Sifu Temple, was the latest filature built in Nanhai. Their second target would be Jichanglong, owned by Qiyuan, who first introduced filature to Nanhai County, helped others to set up filatures and took away their livelihood.[10]

At the festival, fueled by heavy drinking and gambling, the weavers' ugly mood and emotional tension rose to a fever pitch. When the diretor of Jingluntang saw the right moment, he began to incite the weavers to destroy Yuhouchang. Soon everyone shouted, "Down with Yuhouchang!" More than 1,000 weavers, carrying knives, swords, hoes, rods, and whatever weapons available, even guns, marched angrily and noisily down the country road to Xuetang village, which was only about 2.5 kilometers away.[11] They were shouting and swearing and at the same time waving the banners of Jingluntang.

The Chen brothers, owners of Yuhouchang, had refused to give a day off to the workers to attend this festival. As the boisterous, unruly mob stomped down the road, the workers in Yuhouchang, mostly female, were working as usual. When the enraged gang broke into the filature, the workers of Yuhouchang ran away for fear of their lives. The mob of weavers became uncontrollable. They smashed the machines one after another and looted 10,000 *piculs* of cocoons and other materials.[12]

When the owners of Yuhouchang got the news, they immediately formed a militia of 20 to 30 men from the village. Armed with broadswords and guns, they hurried to the village gate and guarded the entrance. During the scuffle that followed, the militia, because of their weapons and training, gained the upper hand, and they drove the mob of weavers out of the village. In the end, two weavers were captured and two others were drowned in the fish ponds.[13]

The weavers, who were driven out of Xuetang village, were furious. Destroying the machines in Yuhouchang was not good enough for them. With more weavers freshly arriving from the temple, they paraded down the road to Jiancun, intending to destroy the machines in Jichanglong, the seat of all their troubles.[14] Jiancun was separated from Xuetang village by the Guanshan River (官山河), which was about 20 to 30 meters wide. Across the river were rice fields, dikes, and ponds without any road directly to Jiancun. If they wished to reach Jiancun by road, they would have to turn back to Guanshanxu (官山墟) and walk westward.

When Qiyuan heard the awful news that Yuhouchang had been attacked and ransacked, he immediately assembled all the young men in the village. He allocated four men with guns to guard the back entrance to the village, another four to patrol the village, and 10 men to secure the west side of River Guanshan to ensure no one would disembark there. Qiyuan stood right in the front entrance to the village gate, holding and waving the seven-star banner of Guanyunzhang (關雲長), which he borrowed from the Guande Temple (關帝廟), hoping to derive the divine power from the deified hero of the Three Kingdoms. Qiyuan's two adult sons and eight other young men carrying guns stood on either side of him. The rest of the young men, about 100 or so, carrying weapons of all sorts, stood on guard behind. To complete the preparation of defense, two small, locally-made cannons were placed prominently at the forefront. Qiyuan did not forget to inform both the local authorities and the army in

Guanshan barracks, asking for help to suppress the impending armed conflict.[15]

Soon the rowdy weavers carrying clubs, swords, and some even with guns, arrived at Jiancun. Seeing the serious display of armed force, they stopped about 100 feet in front of the village gate. More and more weavers arrived. Some climbed up the Xiqiao Mountain to have an overview of the defense and realized that any forced entrance to the village would incur injury and even death. They hesitated.

Qiyuan reasoned with the weavers that his main motive of establishing the filature in Jiancun was to develop the economy in the village so that everyone could have a better life. During the past eight years they had coexisted peacefully and most people in the village were no longer hungry. Qiyuan carried on to explain that the scarcity of cocoons that year was due to bad weather and a poor harvest, and that they should sit down and discuss how to solve the current problem rather than resorting to violence. He urged them to go home and let the government deal with the situation.

These words fell on deaf ears because the weavers were of firm conviction that the filatures took away their jobs. They refused to go away.[16] The day had been long, and the sun began to set, cooling off both the heat and the anger. After they heard that two of their comrades had been arrested and two drowned, the weavers finally came to a sensible decision to leave for the day. Overnight, the villagers of Xuetang built fortifications guarding the roads leading to the village and delivered the two prisoners to the county authorities.

The owners of Yuhouchang reported the incident to Xu Gengbi (徐賡陛), the Nanhai County magistrate. After reading the reports from the owners of Yuhouchang and Chen Qiyuan, Xu recognized the seriousness of the situation. The following day, (14 August), over 2,000 weavers again marched to Xuetang village. Xu sent in local militia to stop them from entering the village and arrested some of the weavers. That same evening, Xu Gengbi took a fast boat to Guangzhou to request an urgent meeting with his superior, the governor of Guangdong and Guangxi Province, to deal with the crisis.[17]

The governor agreed with him on the urgency and the significance of the situation as there were over 10,000 weavers in Nanhai County and more in the neighboring counties of Shunde and Sanshui. They knew that about 15 years ago, in 1866, a mob of weavers had demonstrated in front of the headquarters of the governor, demanding the annulment of the *likin* tax. In 1875, another mob of weavers smashed the sedan chair of the county magistrate. Both the county magistrate and the governor desperately wanted to avoid recurring trouble from the weavers. Xu Gengbi suggested applying the following measures to the weavers' guild and the owners of filatures. He would release most of arrested men but would order the executions of the four instigators of the attack on Yuhouchang. He would place all weavers under a *baojia* system and demand monthly reports on their activities. Every 10 weavers were to be organized under one foreman and all weavers in a village under a headman, who would guarantee the behavior of the weavers, and in turn, owners of weaving shops would guarantee the behavior of the headman. On the other side, Xu recommended permanent closure of all filatures because, as prescribed by law, all industrial enterprises in China were run under government supervision; private industrial enterprises were unlawful. In the current dispute, he believed that the owners of the 10 filatures had robbed the livelihoods of thousands of weavers.[18]

The governor agreed with both proposals from Xu. To help Xu to suppress further riots, the governor ordered two companies of soldiers to go to Nanhai as soon as possible. Together with another company of soldiers under the command of Xu Gengbi, there would be a total of 1,500 soldiers on site to deal with possible violence.[19] On receiving the verbal agreement of the governor, Xu immediately left Guangzhou. When he arrived at Nanhai County the following day on 15 August, he wasted no time preparing the proclamation of his plan of closing all 10 filatures as the way to solve the conflict.

The weavers of Jingluntang realized that their lack of firearms had thwarted their entry to Xuetang village. On 14 August, they demanded that the owners of weavers' shops donate funds for the purchase of firearms, and they collected over 1,000 *taels* of silver. On 15 August, Jingluntang requested all its members to stay off work and wait for further orders. They congregated at the temple for prayers to remember their dead brothers and vowed to wipe out

Xuetang village the next day. Knowing that the fight could not be avoided, Xuetang elders immediately notified Xu Gengbi of the impending attack. At the same time, they sent women and children away with their valuables and requested assistance from the militia of nearby villages. They vowed to defend their own village.[20]

To diffuse the situation, Xu Gengbi posted his proclamation on 16 August in all the villages in Xiqiao and in neighboring villages, while simultaneously ordering the closure of the 10 filatures immediately and permanently.[21] At the same time, he sent the village elders to the temple to inform the weavers of the government's decision to close the filatures and that they should leave the temple for home. The decision to close the filatures, however, did not satisfy all the weavers. Two thousand of them refused to go away until each machine in every filature in the county had been destroyed.[22]

In the afternoon of 18 August, around 3,000 weavers, some armed with guns, surrounded Xuetang village. They fired guns to force entry. Xuetang villagers, fully prepared for the assault, fired back. Luckily the two companies of soldiers sent by the governor had arrived. All three companies of soldiers moved in quickly to Xuetang village. The weavers retreated, knowing that they could not fight against professional soldiers.[23]

The Silk Weavers' Riot (sometimes known as the Xuetang Riot) in 1881 ended with the closure of all filatures in the county of Nanhai and the instigators of the riot executed.

The Closure of the Filature

The forced closure of Chen Qiyuan's filature and other filatures in Nanhai sparked a series of debates in the Chinese newspaper, *Shenbao* (申報) in Shanghai. At that time, Chinese silk merchants vehemently opposed the founding of filatures claiming that the silk filatures were robbing the weavers of their income from silk reeling, and that the female workers living in a residence in Shanghai would lead to immoral practices. Thus, these merchants urged the filatures to be closed. Others defended the establishment of filatures just as forcefully. One editorialist pointed out that the filatures brought in more opportunities for the cocoon producers to expand business and provided more work for women and unemployed workers in the hinterland.[24] Another editorialist invoked the Confucian doctrine that rulers should seek to improve the welfare of all people, not that of a few individuals nor of one profession.[25]

The Self-Strengthening Movement in China, which began in the 1860s after the Second Opium War, mainly involved modernization of military defense, but some attention was also given to commerce, industry, and agriculture. The Qing Government sanctioned what was known as "government-supervised merchant undertakings." These were profit-oriented enterprises, which were operated by merchants but controlled by government officials. The capital for these enterprises came from private sources; the government provided subsidies in some cases and supervised their operation. An excellent example was the China Merchants' Steam Navigation Company Ltd., established in 1872, which benefited from official patronage, particularly from Li Hongzhang. Government assistance included remission of taxes, loans, interest deferral, and granting of monopoly on transporting tribute gains and official goods. Petitions by other Chinese merchants to establish steamship companies for both inland and overseas shipping were repeatedly rejected by Li, who jealously guarded the privileges enjoyed by the Chinese Merchants' Steam Navigation Company.[26] Private enterprises were thus strongly discouraged.

All filatures in Nanhai were private enterprises and therefore illegal. They were also considered as the cause of the Xuetang Riot. Xu Gengbi, the county magistrate, was not a corrupt official as many were then. Like other officials, he did not want any trouble. He saw closing all filatures as the easiest way to end the weavers' riot. Xu cited that the filatures not only violated the law, but also robbed the livelihood of thousands of people.[27] On the other hand, if there had been no complaints, he would have turned a blind eye to the filatures; after all, the filatures brought prosperity to the region and increased government revenue.

This incident has been viewed as an example of the interference of bureaucratic conservatism in the development of modern industry, in the name of preventing civil disturbance and preserving official monopoly. It has also been considered as a concrete case of conflict between modern industry and traditional handicrafts.

Qiyuan had no option but to close the filature, as did the owners of the nine others. He was most disappointed to see his invention and his enormous efforts of 15 years wiped out by the closure order. He was even more distressed when the owners of these filatures who had humbly asked him for advice and for the blueprints of his machines before, now pointed their fingers at him and blamed him for their financial loss. But the workers of the filatures in his village and those nearby lost their jobs with the closure order, and their livelihood had been robbed in favor of the interests of the weavers. They were most sympathetic towards Qiyuan.

The closure order did not upset Qiyuan for long. After a great deal of thought, Qiyuan decided to move the filature to Macau. He had considered Shunde and Sanshui, where a number of filatures had already sprung up and operating. But those villages were still within Guangdong, and the law restricting private enterprises could always be applied. Moreover, Qiyuan did not want to compete with the existing filatures. He had also considered Hong Kong, but it was too far from the silkworm cultivation region, and transportation would be expensive. He finally settled for Macau, a Portuguese colony, which is closer to Nanhai.[28]

The Interlude in Macau

In the latter half of the fifteenth century, there was an expedition fever at sea in Europe. The stories of Marco Polo's travels aroused the interest of many to find the sea route to China to trade. The Portuguese traders were the first to arrive at the coast of Guangdong at the beginning of the sixteenth century, but they were not allowed to stay. Despite being turned away many times, they kept coming back. After a shipwreck near Macau, they built sheds there to dry their goods, then they built houses as residences, and gradually, they established themselves in Macau. Their residence was never officially authorized by the Qing government. Macau rapidly became the nexus in Portugal's trade along three major routes: Macau-Malacca-Lisbon; Guangzhou-Macau-Nagasaki; and Macau-Manila-Acapulco. Both Chinese and Portuguese merchants flocked to Macau, and trade thrived between 1580 and 1630s. After 1637, Japan sealed itself off from all foreign influence, and trade between Japan and China was severed. In 1685, the privileged position of the Portuguese in trade with China ended following a decision by the emperor of China to allow Chinese to trade with all foreign countries.[29] After 1842, when Hong Kong was ceded to the British, Macau's position as a major regional trading center further declined. During the 19th century, when many Chinese emigarated to other countries as laborers or coolies, Macau was, for a short period of time, an important transit port until 1870, when this function was overtaken by Hong Kong. In the 1850s, the Portuguese government legalized gambling in Macau, making it the "Gambling Capital of the World" or the "Monte Carlo of the Orient." Gambling is currently Macau's biggest source of revenue, making up about 50% of the economy.[30]

Since the laws and regulations in Macau were different from laws in China, it would be difficult for a stranger who was not a resident to start a factory in a foreign land where he had no connections. Qiyuan was introduced to Lu Jiu (盧九), a well-established and well-connected man in the gambling business in Macau.³¹ When Lu Jiu learned of Qiyuan's plight, he was more than willing to help. Lu Jiu felt that the Qing government's loss would be Macau's gain. Macau would benefit from having a filature.

To move the filature to Macau required about 6,000 to 7,000 *taels* of silver. Jichanglong had stopped operating for a few months by then. Qiyuan had to ask Qishu in Annam for financial help. The move was by no means easy. Finding a suitable workforce had always been problematic and yet most crucial for the productivity of the filature. With great difficulties, Qiyuan and his two loyal staff, Ah Fu and Ah Liang, recruited a workforce of about 80, 20 of whom were from Jiancun and the rest from neighboring counties.³² The filature, located on Erlonghou Garden Road (二龍喉花園馬路) which began operation in 1882, was much smaller than Jichanglong, employing about 100 people. Qiyuan named the filature Hechang (和昌),³³ meaning peace and prosperity; later, he renamed it Fuhelong (復和隆), meaning restoration of peace and prosperity.³⁴ Two months after the filature had opened and was working well, Qiyuan left it in the hands of his two loyal staff, Ah Fu and Ah Liang. He hurried back to Jiancun, anxious to start another project which had been in his head for a while.

Fuhelong made only a small profit because of the higher cost of cocoon transportation and the added cost of providing room and board for workers recruited from outside Macau. To entice female workers from Jichanglong, Qiyuan had to offer a higher wage. It is also possible that the reduced profit was due to a percentage of the earnings being distributed to Lu Jiu and He Lianwang (何連旺), who had helped him to set up the filature in Macau. The latter was the son of He Gui (何桂), another business tycoon in Macau, who owned several casinos and a number of other ventures.[35] It was customary at that time for casino owners in Macau to invest in various business enterprises, such as tobacco, cement, tea, and silk.[36]

Fuhelong reeled silk according to two specifications, one for export to the United States and the other to European countries. Its quality was good for export. The growth of the business of Fuhelong was not as rapid as Jichanglong, which Qiyuan had indicated by stating that his silk business "had declined dramatically." However, in July 1884, He Lianwang applied to the Macau government to improve and enhance the drainage system of Fuhelong—a sign of flourishing business, requiring lots of water. After Qiyuan had moved his filature back to Jiancun in 1885, He Lianwang applied for the reopening of the filature in 1890, suggesting that silk business had been reasonably profitable.[37]

After Qiyuan had moved his filature to Macau, three other filatures from Nanhai District followed hot on his heels, bringing jobs to the local population and revenue to the government coffers.[38]

The "Bicycle Silk Reeling Machine"

In Macau, away from Jiancun, Qiyuan examined his project in Jiancun critically and in a more dispassionate way. Although his project did improve the economy and provided the peasants with adequate food, clothing, and even some savings, it simultaneously took away the livelihood of the weavers and the hand-reelers by competing for cocoon supply. Moreover, Chinese people in those days were strictly bound by traditional Confucian ethics, which dictated that "it is improper for men and women to touch each other's hand in giving or receiving an item (男女授受不親)," known as the teaching of Mencius (孟子).[39] Employing women alongside men in a factory setting was frowned upon by many. A solution had to be found to enable women to continue to reel silk at home and at the same time to produce silk of sufficiently good quality for export purposes.

Qiyuan rationalized that the most important technological advances to produce good quality reeled silk were the inclusion of the twisting mechanism using one of the two methods, the Chambon or the Tavelle system, and the heating of cocoons to an optimal temperature to soften the sericin by steam rather than by charcoal to prevent pollution of the reeled silk. A simple and inexpensive reeling machine with a single basin for domestic use, incorporating these two features to produce good quality silk, powered by foot treadle, would be an ideal way to solve the problem. There should be no reason for the government to ban the use of such a machine at home.

Qiyuan asked his second son (third-born), Puxuan, who had talents like his father, to design such a machine. Puxuan had accompanied his father to Jichanglong since it opened and had learned about silk reeling machines. Delighted by the challenge, Puxuan turned Jichanglong, which was then half empty, into his workshop, working away with great enthusiasm.[40]

Soon he came up with a design. Father and son poured over it and agreed that it would work. The machine, using the Chambon twisting mechanism, would be powered by a foot treadle using human energy and should not be banned by the government (Figure 5.1, 5.2). To obtain good quality silk, steam was used to heat up the water in the basin containing the cocoons. Steam was generated by a small boiler and carried by a pipe to the basin to heat up the water.

Figure 5.1. "Bicycle silk reeling machine" for domestic use, displayed in Chen Qiyuan Memorial Hall (photo by May Kaan)

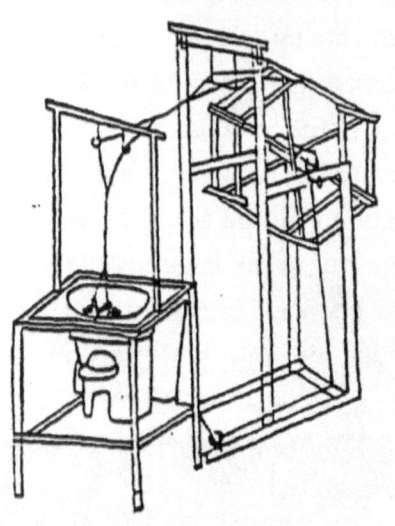

Figure 5.2. Diagram of "bicycle silk reeling machine in Chen Qiyuan's book *Can Sang Pu*, 2015, 86

The machine passed the crucial test of producing as good quality silk as filature silk, although it was not as efficient as the multi-basin machines used in the filature. Qiyuan called this the "bicycle silk reeling machine".[41] It was inexpensive (only about HK$10),[42] structurally simple, and easily reproduced.

The newly designed machine caused a great deal of interest and commotion. Farmers from Jiancun and neighboring villages lined up to have a look at the new invention. The amount of investment could vary greatly, from purchasing one machine for home use to 10 to 20 machines for a small workshop. It was highly suitable for the needs of the rural community. Just like his father, Puxuan carefully and patiently explained the workings of the machine to the customers. For those who wanted to make the machines, he freely provided blueprints. With the help of a few technicians, Puxuan turned the half-empty Jichanglong into a filature using the "bicycle silk reeling machines" to produce reeled silk. Qiyuan named the filature Lizhen Silk Filature (利貞絲廠).[43]

The bicycle silk reeling machine accomplished two goals. It was compatible with a more decentralised form of production, boosting the growth of small-scale local entrepreneurs who established foot-powered workrooms. It also prolonged the existence of home reeling. In retrospect, it seems that Qiyuan should have reversed the order, to have introduced the "bicycle silk reeling machines" first, which was readily accepted by the rural community, and might have prevented the silk weavers' riot. Establishing filatures, which would invariably bring about significant social changes, later might have been more easily accepted by the local people after they were accustomed to new technology and saw the necessity for advancement.

When Qiyuan hurried home after the opening of the new filature in Macau, he found, as expected, that that year Nanhai was blessed with a good harvest of cocoons, and the supply of cocoons greatly exceeded the demand because of the closure of 10 filatures. This excess production drove the price of cocoons down and those engaged in sericulture suffered. Despite the increasing use of the "bicycle silk reeling machine," there was still an excess of cocoons in the market the following year.

After a while, some filatures quietly resumed operation on a smaller scale. Since cocoons were plentiful, the weavers did not complain. The closure of filatures had caused hardship for those who lost their jobs; some were relatives and friends of the weavers, while the government lost almost one million *taels* of silver in tax revenue. Since there was no complaint, the government turned a blind eye to the illegal re-establishment of filatures in Nanhai. Seeing no action from the government, more filatures reopened one by one. Even Chen Jinqiong (陳錦筇), son of Qishu, established a new filature named Lihousheng (利厚生), employing steam-powered multi-basin reeling machines which operated side by side with Puxuan's filature using "bicycle silk reeling machines".[44]

In 1885, Qiyuan decided to move the Macau filature, Hechang, back to Jiancun. Some said that the decision was made after Qiyuan received an invitation from the Qing officials to return. In 1887, the ban on filatures was officially lifted as a result of government's change of policy dictated by the Self-Strengthening Movement. Private enterprise was then encouraged.[45] The number of filatures mushroomed following the lifting of the ban. China's silk industry reached its height in the late 1910s and early 1920s. The Pearl River Delta prospered with the rising silk industry and trade, which in turn led to development of other industries and trade. Qiyuan consolidated all three filatures, Licheng, Lihousheng, and Hechang, in one place and called it

Sichanglun (世昌綸), which had 500 basins, and later increased to 800.⁴⁶ Since then, the silk export business in the Pearl River Delta Region blossomed.

Sichanglun continued to operate until 1928 when it closed its doors as a result of the decline of the silk industry in China.

Chapter 6: Accomplishments in Later Years (1885 to 1904)

Figure 6.1. Chen Qiyuan

By the time Jichanglong reopened in Jiancun in 1885, Chen Qiyuan (Fig. 6.1) was over 50 years of age. He married his first wife (Figure 6.2) in 1853 before he left for Annam. She gave birth to four children, two boys and two girls. Qiyuan's second wife gave birth to one son, and his third wife to two (one died in infancy). By the time Qiyuan was in Macau, the second and third wives had already passed away. He was actively looking for another wife while he was in Macau. In

1886, he married his fourth wife in Macau, who bore him three children, of which one girl died in infancy. A capable woman, his fourth wife (Figure 6.3) helped him not only at home but also acted as a supervisor in the factory in Macau, gaining the trust and respect of the female workforce.[1] His youngest son (ninth-born) was born in 1890 when Qiyuan turned 54. Altogether Qiyuan had five sons and three daughters who survived to adulthood (Figure 2.1). The oldest son was 35 years older than the youngest, which was not unusual in the old days in China when polygamy was legal.

Figure 6.2. Chen Qiyuan's first wife (left) and fourth wife (right)

After Qiyuan reopened Jichanglong and amalgamated the two smaller filatures called Lizhen and Lihousheng with it as Sichanglun, his business prospered. He paid close attention to other aspects of the silk business, such as to ensure a good supply of cocoons and export of silk through Changzan Sizhuang, a silk commission house he established in Guangzhou. He continued to help others in establishing silk filatures and silk reeling workshops, using the popular "bicycle silk reeling machines." The silk reeling industry flourished in Nanhai and in Shunde. The amount of reeled silk exported from China increased with time.

While the total raw silk exported from China increased by twofold from around 60,000 piculs in 1873 to around 110,000 in 1901, the increase from Guangzhou was almost fourfold, from 9,600 piculs to 37,000 during the same period (Figure 6.3). The capital investment required for the silk reeling filature designed by Qiyuan was much lower than that required for the steam-powered filature (under 10,000 taels versus 25,000 taels of silver for a filature of 300 employees). The Pearl River Delta area possessed many advantages for the silk industry compared with Yangtze River Delta area (see Chapter 1) and the promotion by Quiyuan and his assistance to other filature owners no doubt contributed to the success. He was pleased to witness in his lifetime the improvement in the standard of living of the natives in his village and the neighboring villages.

年份（公元）	华丝出口量（担）			
	华丝合计	其中：粤丝出口量		
		七里丝	厂丝	小计
1873	6万多			
1883	59,143	8,302	1,254	9,556
1887	66,694	8,462	7,158	15,620
1891	84,948	4,928	10,219	15,147
1897	97,564	1,933	22,727	24,660
1901	108,696	2,375	34,612	36,987

华丝出口量表
This is the list of Chinese silk's export quantity.

Figure 6.3. Export of raw silk from China and from Guangzhou from 1873 to 1901 as displayed at Chen Qiyuan Memorial Hall (photo by David Yeung)

Chen Qiting Ancestral Hall and Distribution of the Estate

While happy and contented to see that his efforts and his work proved fruitful, Qiyuan began to delegate the task of running the family business to his sons and nephews. He believed that after the age of 50, one should "retire" from business. There was something on his mind that needed his urgent attention. When Qiyuan and Qishu left for Annam after the death of their father, they had decided that the estate of their father would remain intact, and they worked together to keep the family going. Whatever profits they made would be divided equally into three portions, one for each family. Now that his brothers had passed away, Qiyuan became the sole head of the Chen family. As his children and the children of his brothers had all grown up by then and some had their own families, it was about time to divide his father's estate, which had grown tremendously under his and his brother's management.

Before Oiyuan divided the family assets, he decided to build an ancestral hall in honor of his grandfather, Chen Qiting. The hall could be used for the younger generations to worship their ancestors, for the members of the Chen clan to connect with each other, and as a place for family and community functions, such as weddings, funerals, and social meetings. In addition, he built 17 detached houses around the ancestral hall, each with a bedroom and a living room as a residence for each member of the family up to the second generation (one for each of the three brothers or their widows and one for each of their sons). The compound was enclosed by a wall with an archway at the entrance. He named the compound Baiyufang (百豫坊). On the surface, the two words Baiyu (百豫) mean one hundred happiness, but according to Chen Zuohai, grandson of Chen Qiyuan, who researched I Ching, The Book of Changes (易經), the following explanation for these two words was given: "Even though one is wealthy, one needs to save; even though one has great achievements, one needs to be humble"—most appropriate in reflecting Chen Qiyuan's thought and behavior. The key component of Chinese society is the family, which includes three of the five ethically important "Confucian human relations:" father and son, husband and wife, and the relationship between siblings (the other two being rulers and subjects, and the relationship between friends). Due to this emphasis on the family, it was customary for the Chinese, even with grown children of their own, to remain close to each other, and sometimes for several generations, to live under the same roof. Qiyuan merely abided by this traditional Chinese custom.[2]

He also purchased several acres of land around Baiyufang to be owned by the Chen clan and managed by one of its members. The rent or profits from the land would be used to pay for the management and repair of the ancestral hall and annual worship. Again, he was following the usual Chinese customs. Wealthy clans often also provided money for the education of the children of the clan.

All the remaining assets (shops and properties), whether in Jiancun, Guangzhou, Annam, or Hong Kong, would be evaluated and divided into three equal portions. For the individuals already managing the shops and would like to continue to manage them, they could do so. The family of Qiyuan's second brother would choose first, followed by the family of the first brother. He would take the remaining portion. Each portion would be evaluated again to make sure that it would approximately amount to one-third. Every member of the family felt that the division was most fair and appropriate, and it was carried out quickly and efficiently without any dispute.[3]

For Qiyuan himself, he further divided his portion into five, one-fifth for each of his four sons (his ninth and youngest son was not yet born at that time). He retained one-fifth for his own use.

百豫坊清代水井

Figure 6.4. The picture of the well of Baiyufang displayed in Chen Qiyuan Memorial Hall (photo by author)

When Baiyufang was completed, Chen chose a most propitious day for the opening of the compound and the placing of the ancestral tablets in appropriate places on the altar. The Chen clan gathered together to worship and give thanks to their ancestors for their protection. Qiyuan announced the method and process of division of assets among the three brothers or their descendants was to be witnessed by village elders. The ceremony was followed by a huge, sumptuous banquet, one that had not been seen in the village for a long time.

Baiyufang belongs to history now. All its living quarters and walls collapsed after the Second World War. The only building standing is Chen Qiting Ancestral Hall, which was converted into Chen Qiyuan Memorial Hall in 1994. The use of granite for building the foundation, the pillars and the floor, and the best quality bricks for erecting the walls, accounted for the sturdiness of the ancestral hall. The walls and the roof were adorned with beautifully carved figurines, as were the panels of the doors opening into the courtyard (see Introduction).

Philanthropic Activities

Even before he returned to Jiancun from Annam, Qiyuan had established meat and grocery shops to provide food at a low price for the villagers. He also opened a rice store, called Yongshenghao (永生號) in Guanshanxu, near Jiancun, to sell rice imported from Vietnam and other daily necessities. He gave free rice subsidies of 20 catties (斤, one catty = 1.323 pounds) each month, to the elderly, the widows, the disabled, and the poor in Jiancun and in two nearby villages, Xingtou (杏頭) and Longreng (龍仍). Each recipient was given a small "rice book" with his or her name, a record of the date, and the amount of rice they received from the store each time. Many received over 20 years of free rice and over 1,000 people had received and used their own "rice book."[4]

Since the mid-Qing Dynasty, there had been a shortage of rice grown in Guangdong because of the expansion of the silk industry. Peasants turned their rice field into mulberry dike-fish ponds for sericulture as this "cash crop" brought in more income than rice. Rice had to be imported. The free rice helped the poor and those in need.

Free Medicine and Burial

In Guanshanxu, Qiyuan opened a herbal medicine store, named Shoushitang (壽世堂), and hired a Chinese medicine practitioner for the sick. For the poor, the store provided free consultations and free medicine. For those who died leaving their relatives unable to afford burial expenses, Qiyuan offered to pay coffin and burial fees. This service had been greatly appreciated by the villagers.[5] In fact, Qiyuan assumed some of the functions of social welfare services of today.

Free Education for Children from Poor Families

Qiyuan taught in the *si-shu* that his father had founded in Jiancun. It was often a hardship for poor families to send their children to a *si-shu* as they could ill afford the fees, which were one tael of silver per annum. Instead, many children at a young age started to work on the farm. They were illiterate and unable to perform very simple arithmetic. Qiyuan rented a space, hired a teacher, and offered free education to children in Jiancun and the two nearby villages, Xingtou and Jishui (吉水), whose parents could not afford to send them to *a si-shu*. Qiyuan called the school Keqin Yixue (克勤義學). Books, paper, pens, brushes, abacuses, and other stationery were also given free to the students.[6]

Along with the usual curriculum offered traditionally by *si-shu*s, he introduced more modern and practical aspects of education. In addition to reading and writing, the children were required to learn how to use the abacus and memorize its formulae, along with basic mathematics including the multiplication table and the use of Arabic numbers in calculations. At a later stage, he hired another teacher and divided the children into two levels: lower and upper, depending on their achievements. Before graduation, the children must be able to read newspapers, write letters and do simple bookkeeping and accounting. Armed with these skills, they would be able to make a living in urban settings, for which they were forever grateful.[7]

Public Dike Repair and Flood Prevention

The River Jishui runs from west to east passing through Jiancun, Xingtou, and Jishui villages before emptying into the Guanshan River. Where several small rivers met, the government of the Ming Dynasty had installed a watergate called Jishui Antrum (吉水竇) (Figure 6.5).

During the rainy season, the gate was left open for excess water to be drained to the sea to avoid flooding of the low-lying areas around Mount Xiqiao. During the dry season, the gate was closed to allow water to accumulate to be used for irrigation. After more than 200 years, part of the structure had collapsed with the gate partly broken because of weathering and lack of repair. The broken watergate was a source of anxiety for people in the nearby villages. If the gate were to break down completely, there would be irreparable damage to the nearby land. Qiyuan submitted a petition to the county magistrate stating the urgent need for Jishu Antrum to be repaired.

吉水窦
Jishui Antrum

Figure 6.5. Picture or Jishui antrum displayed at Chen Qiyuan Memorial Hall (photo by May Kaan)

The repair work for Jishui Antrum required 5,000 *taels* of white silver. The county magistrate recognized the urgency of the problem but did not have such a huge sum in the county coffer. He could only spare 200 *taels* of silver and would authorize repairs to be carried out if money could be raised. After thinking about the problem, Qiyuan agreed to lead the project. He organized a meeting of the leaders of the villages that might be affected by the Jishui Antrum. The villages were poor and could only raise 800 *taels* of silver among them. Including the 200 *taels* of silver from the county magistrate, the total came to 1,000 *taels* of silver. It was during the early days of operation of Jichanglong when expansion demanded more capital investment and other philanthropic activities also required support. Qiyuan could only donate 1,000 *taels* of silver. He finally arrived at the following arrangement: he would provide the leadership, the technical know-how, and 1,000 *taels* of silver, but the villages would provide the needed labor. The 2,000 *taels* of silver raised would be used to purchase materials for repair and he would cover any excess cost.[8] The village came up with a timetable of contribution to voluntary labor. Under the leadership and supervision of Qiyuan, the repair work was completed in two years. Qiyuan also utilized the labor provided by the community to repair the embankment in the surrounding low-lying areas to prevent flooding of rice fields, a much less costly job than the repair of Jishui watergate, but just as useful.[9]

At the end of these two projects, the peasants in the nearby villages were relieved of the fear and anxiety of impending flood and damages to their properties. The mulberry dike-fish ponds and the land along Jishu River flourished. Qiyuan contributed not only funds, but his time, energy, and technical knowledge to these two public service projects. His efforts were greatly appreciated by the peasants and they thanked the "Seventh Master," (Qiyuan was seventh among the siblings in his family), heartily for his efforts and generosity.[10]

Charity Halls

Qiyuan established the first charity hall in Guanshanxu named Puji (普濟善堂, Universal Charity Hall). Puji functioned as a private charity organization giving free medical consultations, medicine, and alms to the poor, the sick, and the disabled. Additionally the organization helped the victims of natural disasters, offered free coffins and free burials to those whose families could not afford it, dealt with the "dumped" bodies[11] on the streets, and provided shelter for unwanted infants left on the streets.

Later, Qiyuan and his friend Chen Jijian (陳景建) founded the Chongzheng Charity Hall (崇正善堂) in Guangzhou. Towards the end of the Qing Dynasty, there were 15 such charity halls in Guangzhou,[12] of which Chongzheng was one of the more well-known ones which were located in populous and industrialized areas. Most of the charity halls were established by chambers of commerce and supported by the wealthy elite. Located in the eleventh district of Xiquan,[13] Chongzheng Charity Hall was run by merchants according to its constitutions. The organization was funded and directed by the merchants and the elite, independent of the government. One of the main functions of Chongzheng was to look after unwanted children, and it became known for its excellent pediatric care.[14] In the past, there were very few hospitals in China, and few people could afford to consult private medical practitioners. The waiting time in clinics in charity halls was long. Sometimes patients waited two to three days without being seen. Chongzheng Charity Hall set up clinics, hired many well-known medical practitioners, and donated medications for the poor. Chongzheng eventually became the Fourth Clinic of Guangzhou Federation of Charity Organizations.[15]

In order not to deplete the charity funds raised, the wealthy elite used their business acumen to invest the donated funds wisely in order to generate interests for operatimg the charity halls, while keeping the principal untouched. Chen Qiyuan in later years was to become the chairman of the Federation of Charity Organizations, responsible for its budget and its investment.[16]

During his lifetime, Qiyuan involved himself in many types of charity work. He donated generously to help victims of disasters and to worthwhile projects to improve the lives of the villagers. After his death, a large part of his estate was donated to charity by his son Puxuan, in accordance with his will.

Scholarly Achievements

Qiyuan did not receive a formal university education or even secondary school education as we have today. He had only a formal primary school education from his father's *si-shu* and the rest was self-taught. Despite failing twice in the "Child Examination," he continued to study a fair number of other books. He was a wizard with the abacus and excelled in mathematics. He was able to fix clocks and watches without any help. In his thirties when he was already wealthy, he spent six years learning physics, mechanics, and steam engines, without much outside guidance. Although he had no formal training or formal degree in mechanics or engineering, he designed the silk reeling machines that best suited the needs of his village. He supervised the repair of Jishu Antrum, work suited for a civil engineer. He was able to apply what he had learned and put his knowledge into practical use, more than some graduates of universities. To pass on his knowledge and experience, Qiyuan had written several books, the two most significant of which were about sericulture and mathematics respectively.

Can Sang Pu (蠶桑譜, *On Sericulture*)

In the 1880s Qiyuan found that more cocoons than necessary were required to produce the same quantity of raw silk because many cocoons had to be discarded due to poor quality. Merchants, in their haste to earn money, paid little to no attention to the process of silkworm rearing, which was labor-intensive and required a lot of attention and skill. As a result, the quality of the eggs and larvae deteriorated or became diseased. Environmental conditions, especially temperature, relative humidity, light, and ventilation conditions affect the well-being and survival of silkworms, and these factors require careful control for successful silkworm rearing.

Qiyuan began to learn about silkworm rearing and experimented on various conditions that would improve the quality of cocoon production. In 1886, he published the first edition of *Can Sang Pu* (蠶桑譜, *On Sericulture*)[17] (Figure 6.6) on the practical aspects of silkworm rearing. The book had four editions: 1886, 1893, 1897, and lastly in 1906.[18] It was highly recommended by experts in silkworm rearing.

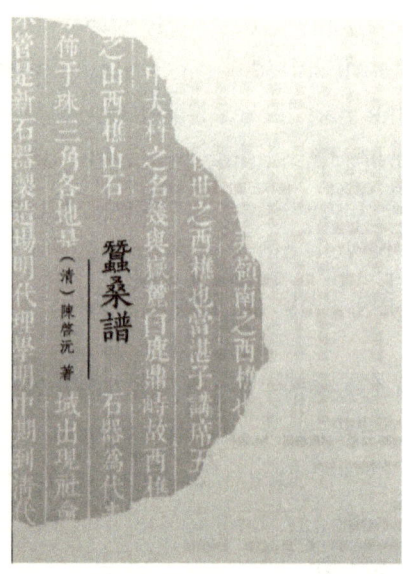

Figure 6.6. Chen Qiyuan's *Can Sang Pu*, (蠶桑譜, *On Sericulture*), Guangxi Normal University Press, 2015

The first and the second editions were published privately. According to Pan Yantong (潘衍桐), who wrote the foreword of the third edition published in 1897, the book had been copied many times and was extensively used in Nanhai and Shunde. Pan Yantong noted that Chen Qiyuan had written the book using language simple enough to be read by those with a primary school education, as most of the villagers were at that time. The third edition of the book was printed by the Government of Guangdong. The fourth edition published in 1906 had the foreword written by Wu Feng (吳對),[19] son of an important minister in the late Qing Dynasty. Wu read the third edition of the book in Tientsin and decided to have another edition printed.[20] The last edition of the book has a brief, two-page autobiography of Qiyuan (Figure 6.7) and two important documentations: an ordinance of the Qing government to allow private ownership of filatures, and a note in 1897 by his fifth son (陳錦簀) recording the shortage of cocoon supply at that time as the main reason for another edition of the book.

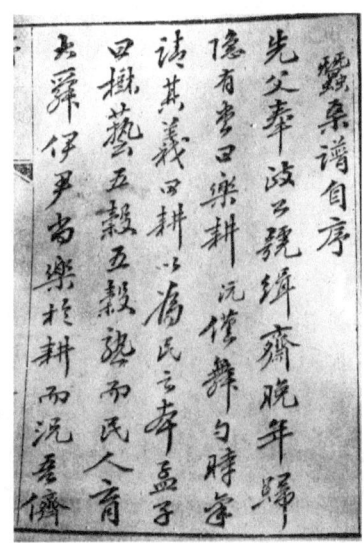

Figure 6.7. First page of Chen Qiyuan's short autobiography in *Can Sang Pu*, 2015, 13–18

The book consists of two parts. The first part provides important information on silkworm rearing: 1) how to recognize the imminent signs of moths breaking out of the cocoons; 2) the importance of preserving good quality eggs for larvae to hatch and the optimal conditions to store the egg sheets (sheets where moths laid their eggs; 3) the likes and dislikes of silkworms (larvae) and how to give optimal care to the silkworms so that they could produce good quality cocoons; and 4) the distinction of good from poor quality cocoons, how to protect the cocoons from flies and ants, and how to maintain an optimal environment for the larvae.

The second part contains information about raw silk production: 1) the method of silk reeling; 2) how to control the temperature of the water for unwinding the silk from the cocoons; 3) how to distinguish good from poor quality silk; and 4) the types of machines available for silk reeling. The rest of the book is devoted to discussion on how to make the conditions more suitable for silkworm rearing and for mulberry cultivation under different weather conditions throughout the year.

The book is unique among literature on the sericulture industry, with much more emphasis on silkworm raising than on mulberry cultivation.[21] Because it is simple and easy to understand, the book satisfied the needs of China's agrarian society and expanded the knowledge of traditional agricultural methods. It was also a reference book for the modern social historians of China. The transmission of knowledge and technology, as a result of the wide circulation of this book, had benefited a large number of people in the silk industry.[22] In 1909, the government of Guangdong, affirming the book to be practical and useful for farmers in sericulture, reprinted 1,000 copies of the book and distributed them widely to all the villages in the Pearl River Delta Region.[23]

Chen Qiyuan's Suan Xue (陳啟沅算學, Chen Qiyuan's Mathematics)

Qiyuan believed that a good understanding of basic mathematics together with efficacious use of the abacus were highly useful for solving day to day problems. He needed the abacus for his daily business transactions. When he had to learn about physics, mechanics, and engineering with the ultimate aim to make the silk reeling machine and the steam engine, he found that mathematics was essential to and inseparable from the above disciplines. In the village school that he sponsored, he made mathematics part of the curriculum so that students who graduated from the school would be able to do simple bookkeeping, a skill useful for any employment opportunity. His own interest in mathematics drove him to write a long treatise on practical and applied mathematics which was published in four volumes in 1889, entitled *Chen Qiyuan's Suan Xue*[24] (陳啟沅算學, *Chen Qiyuan's Mathematics*, Figure 6.8). It took him over 10 years to complete this book. With its heavy emphasis on solving practical problems encountered in everyday life, the book is very different from other mathematic texts which typically emphasize theories and equations.

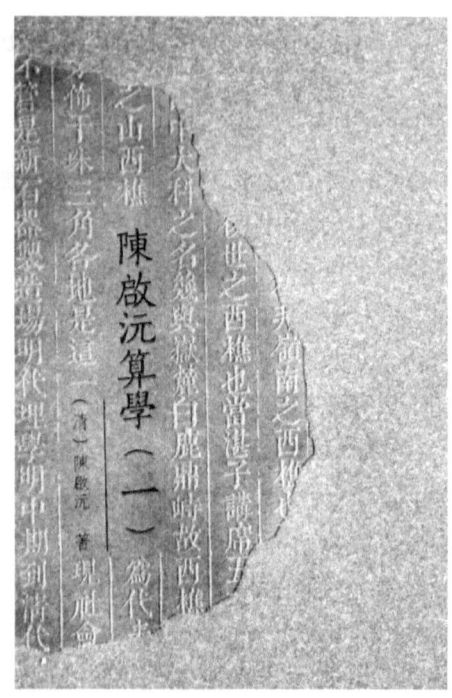

Figure 6.8. Chen Qiyuan's Suan Xue (陳啟沅算學, *Chen Qiyuan's Mathematics*) *Volume 1,* Guangxi: Guangxi Normal University Press, *2015*

The first few chapters of the book illustrated simple, easy-to-solve mathematical problems, while later chapters dealt with more difficult ones. It was clear and allowed people to follow readily. Even after he had completed the book, he kept it for a long time without publishing it. It was only after the manuscript had been borrowed many times by friends and relatives who found it useful and urged him to publish it that he finally put it into print. He worried that the book would invite criticisms from those with a deeper and

162

better understanding of mathematics. He was a humble man and fully aware of his lack of formal education.[25]

Qiyuan's book reflects an accumulation of knowledge of ancient Chinese mathematics that he had learned and used. He used Chinese rather than Arabic numerals and utilized the abacus as a calculator for solving the problems. Calculators and computers were not available in those days.

The book has 13 chapters. Chapters 1 and 2 dealt with the numerals, decimals, measurements, and abacus use. The problems were presented as questions and answers, and examples were drawn from everyday life in the market and in trading at that time. For example, if there were 261 chests of cocoons, and from every nine chests one could obtain one picul of raw silk, how many piculs of raw silk would one get from the 261 chests of cocoons? In Chapter 2, he discussed the issues of investment in the village setting when each villager put in a certain sum of money into a loan fund to generate income or interest. The chapter taught the principle of calculating interest.

Chapters 3 to 9 followed the presentation of the ancient classic Chinese mathematics book, which has remained invaluable to this day, *The Nine Chapters on the Mathematical Art* (九章算術), which had been composed by several generations of scholars from the tenth to second century B.C. and is one of the earliest surviving mathematics books in China. It lays out an approach to mathematics that centers on finding and using the most general method of solving problems. Chen Qiyuan noted in his book some of the errors he found in the ancient text.

Chapters 10 to 12 described the use of geometry in calculating the area and the length of the sides of various shapes. In the last chapter, he discussed the basis and methods of surveying, measurement of air pressure, water pressure, and the ratio and spectrum of mirror images and shadows. This chapter also included the theories behind watch and clock making, the steam engine, the measurement of the speed of light, light refraction, the speed of sound, the principle and use of levers, the use of concave and convex mirrors, the magnifying glass, and various other measuring instruments.

Chen Qiyuan's book on mathematics was, at that time, one of the more comprehensive books on the subject. It contained the curriculum of mathematics comparable to the current-day secondary school level. When the book was published in 1889 in the late Qing Dynasty, reforms in education had begun and a number of schools were using the Western method of teaching. Arabic numerals were used instead of Chinese ones and the abacus was no longer in use in schools. As a result, Qiyuan's book soon became outdated and was not used in the school curriculum.

Qiyuan also wrote a number of other books, of which two were published: *The Origin of Liqi* (理氣溯源) and *Understanding the Theories of I-Ching* (周易理數會通), which was a book on philosophy.[26] Qiyuan spent about 30 years studying feng shui and was a well-known feng shui master. He was an avid reader and interested in a wide variety of subjects. One of his favorite books was on Chinese philosophy: *Hundred Schools of Thought* (諸子百家).[27]

These ancient classics have had a profound influence on Chinese customs, thought, and culture lasting to the present day.

His Special Gift—Unusual Eyesight

Qiyuan was gifted with superior eyesight, far above that of an ordinary person. He had the ability to see colors in the dark, to see things at a great distance without the aid of a telescope, and to detect very small objects without the use of a microscope. Chen Qiyuan had been given a number of nicknames because of his unusual eyesight: "ghost-eyed seven," "ghost-eyed Chen," or "The Unique Fellow of Nanhai" (南海畸人). He was not proud and did not think much of his special talent. He once said, "This unusual gift is only good as a conversational piece. It does not benefit the country or its people."[28] He intended to use this gift to establish something useful and helpful to the people.

There had been many stories of Qiyuan's superior eyesight, passed down the generations in the family. From Hong Kong Island, he could read signboards across the harbor on the Kowloon side. He could read the names carved on tombstones on the mountain side from far away. He was frequently tested by people who did not believe in his unusual capacity. He was able to copy the whole Kangxi Dictionary[29] of over 47,000 characters in microscript on the front and back of a Chinese hand-held fan, thus amply confirming his unusual talent.[30] According to his grandson

Chen Lianzhong (陳廉仲), Qiyuan produced three such fans. One of the fans was given to the county magistrate and another to Chong Qi (崇綺), a Manchurian bannerman, who was a *zhuangyuan* (狀元) in the Chinese Imperial Examination and became the father-in-law of Emperor Tongzhi (同治皇帝). The last fan was donated by Qiyuan's great-grandson to Guangdong Museum during the Cultural Revolution and could no longer be found. One can only presume that it was lost.[32]

Chen Zuohai, Qiyuan's only surviving grandson, had seen his grandfather's microscript fan when he was about 17 years old. It was mounted in a glass frame. On the side of the frame was a magnifying glass to enable people to read the script on the fan. Toward the end of the script, Qiyuan wrote: "I am now getting old and am not be able to do much more. This fan is dedicated to people in the generations to come." This was the last fan that he had worked on.

Qiyuan was not the only one who could do microscript. Several other people had been reported to have such ability. Xie Yuqin (謝玉琴), for example, had written 268 Chinese characters of *Prajnaparamita Hrdaya Sutra* (般若波羅密多心經) on a piece of her mother's white hair; and Wang Zhiwen (王芝文) spent seven years writing 352,963 characters of the *Records of the Three Kingdoms* (三國志) on a porcelain quiver for arrows about three feet in length. Wang also wrote 300 poems of 6,000 characters on a calling card with each character occupying 0.75 square millimeters.[33]

In fact, these people have unusual eyesight like that of an eagle or other birds of prey. Scientists have found that the retina of an eagle's eye, compared with that of the human eye, is more densely coated with the light-detecting cells, called cones, thus enhancing its power to resolve fine details. An eagle can see four to five times further than the human eye can. Furthermore, an eagle's eye is sensitive to dim light, and able to differentiate more shades and colors than the human eye. It is possible that Qiyuan had a great deal more cones in his retina, which could have given him powerful vision and enabled him to see colors in the dark. Unfortunately, this wonderful gift was not hereditary since almost all his descendants have required corrective lenses for myopia.

In those days, there was no electricity, only kerosene or oil lamps, which did not generate adequate light for such delicate work. According to Chen Zuohai, Qiyuan had a small, dark room in his house with no windows, which was separated from the rest of the house so that he could work undisturbed. There was a small opening in the ceiling which allowed a ray of light to come in and shine directly onto a table where he placed the best quality paper to make the fan. Before starting to write on the fan, Qiyuan would burn some incense, sit down and meditate for about half an hour. When his mind had settled down, he began to write the small characters with great concentration so that no mistakes would be made. Making a mistake would mean that the whole process had to be restarted from the beginning.

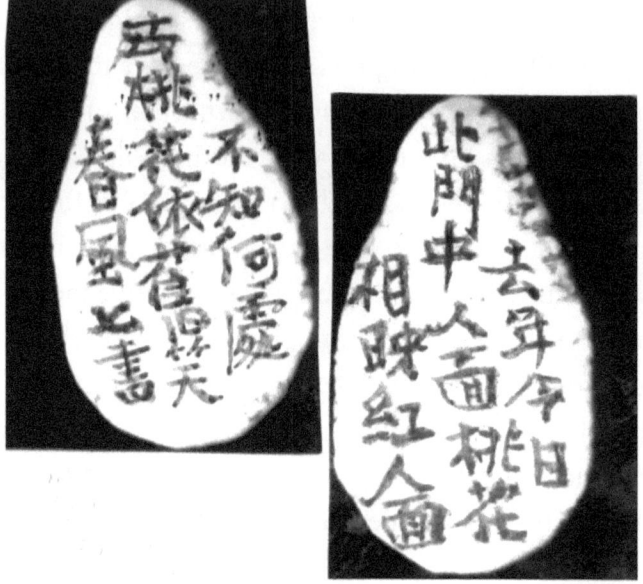

Figure 6.9. Picture of the poem written by Chen Qiyuan on small pieces of ivory, the size of a seasame seed displayed in Chen Qiyuan Memorial Hall (photo by David Yeung)

Obviously, it would not be possible to use an ordinary brush to write characters so small and so clearly. Qiyuan experimented using feathers or hairs of different animals and found that rat hair gave the most satisfactory results.[34] At present, the only existing example or work of micro-writing that is in the possession of his descendants is a poem of 30 characters written on two tiny pieces of ivory, the size of a sesame seed, with an area of 14.44 square millimeters (Figure 6.9).

168

Surveying and Mining

In 1900, Qiyuan received an unexpected summons from the Yamen (衙門) of Governor of Guangxi and Guangdong asking him to resolve a dispute among three mining companies. The Governor at that time was Tao Mo (陶模),[35] who had been unable to end the dispute of three mining companies for a number of years as there was no one in the government with the expertise to solve the issue. The three mining companies had worked alongside each other in peace in Shaoquan (韶關) until the discovery of an antimony lode in that area. All three companies wanted to expand their mining activities into that area. The conflict was over the boundaries of the three properties; each company claimed a different property boundary. The argument had deteriorated to physical violence with injuries and even deaths. To avoid further clashes, the government ordered the suspension of mining in the area. Although this decision stopped the confrontations, the government lost tax revenue.

One of the advisors to Tao Mo's government had read Qiyuan's mathematics book and suggested to the Governor to invite Chen Qiyuan to conduct a proper survey to end the dispute.[36] When Qiyuan received the invitation, he felt honored to have been asked to do such an important job since he was a merchant, the lowest rank in the four social classes. Even though he possessed the instruments and had written about survey, he had no experience in conducting a survey himself. This invitation gave him the opportunity to put the theories into practice. Despite his age (64 years), he accepted the invitation readily. Taking all the necessary equipment with him, such as his version of theodolite (a surveying instrument with a rotating telescope for measuring horizontal and vertical angles), tapes, rods (each 16.5 feet in length), a magnetic compass, and a leveling instrument which he had invented himself, he left home with two assistants on a government boat.

They traveled up the Beijiang arriving in Shaoquan in about three days. On the following day, he met with the officials and the owners of the three mining companies. The area of dispute was a ravine with lots of trees, and the site of the lode of antimony. Qiyuan studied carefully the documentation of the three properties and discovered that a proper survey had not been carried out and property boundaries had not been established.[37]

He started surveying with the help of his two assistants the following day. As this was the first time he conducted an actual survey, he was very excited. Despite the daunting physical work of climbing up the mountain without trails and with lots of trees and shrubs, he carried out the survey energetically and with great precision. Because of his excellent eyesight, there was no need for him to use a telescope. The work proceeded very smoothly and was completed in just over 10 days. He spent another 10 days making the necessary calculations. Then he produced a relief map of the area of dispute, carefully marking the boundaries of the properties of the three mining companies. As a result of the survey, he discovered a piece of land that did not belong to any of the three companies and suggested that this piece of land belong to the government.

About six weeks after his arrival, he was able to submit a comprehensive report to the magistrate of the prefecture of Shaoguan, who was the official responsible for mining. A meeting was organized for Qiyuan to discuss with the owners of the three companies and the relevant government officials to explain to them how the boundaries of the three properties were determined. All three owners were happy with the survey results and agreed on the boundaries determined. The officials then placed stone markers to show the limit of each property.[38]

Grateful for the amiable ending of the dispute which had gone on in acrimony for so many years, the county magistrate sent Qiyuan off with a huge banquet and a laudatory report to the Governor of Guangxi and Guangdong praising Qiyuan for his scientific methods in resolving the dispute. Chen Qiyuan became well-known among the Guangxi and Guangdong government circles. Realizing the lack of technical expertise in his administration, Tao Mo, the Governor, appreciated very much the work of Qiyuan. He knew of Qiyuan's achievement in inventing the silk reeling machines which boosted the economy of the province and the government's tax revenue and wanted to recognize his contributions. He met with Qiyuan personally and complimented Qiyuan on his excellent work and offered him the official honorary title of *Huālíng dào xián* (花翎道銜) (Figure 6.10), but without remuneration or portfolio—a very appropriate recognition since Qiyuan was already 65 years of age and wealthy, but without an official title.

Figure 6.10. The record of Chen Qiyuan's donation using his honorary official title displayed in Chen Qiyuan Memorial Hall (photo by David Yeung)

The governor was looking forward to receiving advice from Qiyuan on other matters that would require scientific and technical input. The honorary appointment also satisfied Qiyuan's needs. Having come from a rural background as a farmer and a merchant, and having failed the Imperial Child Examination twice, Qiyuan steadfastly refused to buy an official title, which was a common practice in those days. When the governor offered Qiyuan the official title, he gladly accepted. The title placed him on a much higher social standing than a farmer or a merchant.[39]

The governor also told him that the appointment would have to come from the Imperial Ministry of Appointment. The Minister at that time was Chong Qi, a scholar and a good friend of the Governor. Qiyuan had just completed a fan with microscript of the Kangxi Dictionary of 47,000 characters. Knowing that Chong Qi was a connoisseur of calligraphy and painting, Qiyuan sent him the fan as a gift.[40]

Three months later, the honorary appointment as a third-rank Qing official *Huālíng Dào Xián* (花翎道銜) came through, complete with an official gown and a hat. In addition, a letter also arrived with a poem composed by Chong Qi, who was 71 years old and indisposed then. His son wrote the letter on his behalf.[41]

The poem (Figure 6.11) can be translated briefly as follows: "In ancient times, there was a man called Li Lou (離婁), who could see clearly at a distance of over 100 steps, and also a man called Gong Shuban (公輸班), who was an excellent craftsman. But since ancient times, there was no one, who had the vision of Li Lou and the skill of Gong Shuban (referring to Qiyuan's superior vision and microscript). Do come and appreciate the unusual treasure from South Guangdong (南粵) (referring to the fan of Qiyuan). You have set your mind on increasing the wealth of the nation and your calligraphy was most unusual. I am glad that your sons are able to inherit your business and are working together to improve the wellbeing of your countrymen."[42].

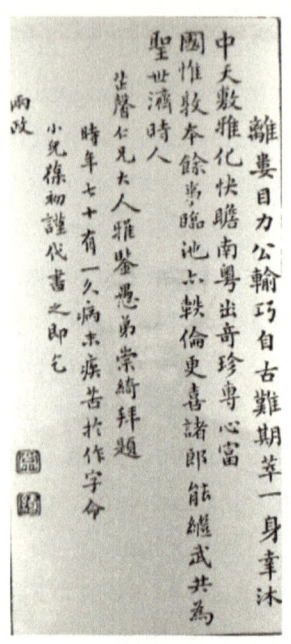

Figure 6.11. Letter from Chong Qi a few months before his death, printed in Chen Qiyuan's *Can Sang Pu*, 2015, 12

    The Governor of Guangxi and Guangdong also granted him the mining rights to the piece of land that Qiyuan discovered that did not belong to the three companies, for a tax-free period of five years. The company had to be self-sufficient as the government would not be responsible for any loss and would not share any profit from the mine. After five years, the government would take over the operation of the mine. Although this appeared to be a generous offer, in reality, the government really wanted Qiyuan to buy the necessary equipment and provide the necessary expertise and labor to start the exploration. It might take two to three years before the mine would become profitable. As expected, the mine began to make some profit after three years. It was returned to the government at the end of five years. By then, Qiyuan had already passed away.[43]

In 1901, silk export from Guangdong had increased so much that the government had a huge surplus. Governor Tao Mo thought about investing in the mining business, and he heard that Tibet was rich in gold deposits. He thought about Qiyuan and requested Qiyuan to investigate the gold mines in Tibet to find out whether any would be worthwhile to purchase. Because of his age, Qiyuan recommended Puxuan to go to Tibet. The Governor agreed. Puxuan spent about six months in Tibet and discovered that although Tibet had a large number of gold deposits, there was no large-scale mining of those rich deposits. When he returned to Guangzhou to report to the governor, Tao Mo had already been replaced. Puxuan brought home a large quantity of Tibetan red flowers, which was said to be able to cure many ailments. The family still has some Tibetan red flowers at present.[44]

In 1904, at the age of 68, Chen Qiyuan passed away.[45] His death was mourned by many, including his family, the natives of Jiancun, and the neighboring villagers. On the day of the funeral, the filature was closed and the farmers also stopped working to pay their last respects to the man who had done so much to improve their lives. Many followed the funeral procession to the burial ground, a place that Chen Qiyuan had chosen himself in Xiǎo Táng Zhè Gū Gǎng (小

塘鷓鴣崗), Nanhai. The tombstone was inscribed by the magistrate of Nanhai County, reading: "The Tomb of the Unique Fellow of Lingnan, Chen Qiyuan" (嶺南畸人陳啟沅之墓).

Chapter 7: Contributions of Chen Qiyuan and their Impact

The first loud shrill up the chimney of Jichanglong, disturbing the tranquility of rural life in Jiancun, signified in a way the arrival of the industrial revolution in South China and changed the lives of people and socioeconomic structures of the silk-producing regions. Chen Qiyuan, who founded the first Chinese silk filature in Jiancun, Nanhai, was responsible for initiating these changes. He was, indeed, a pioneer of modern Chinese industry.

Development of the silk industry and silk export

Chen Qiyuan founded the first silk filature, Jichanglong, in 1874 in Jiancun, Xiqiao, in the Pearl River Delta Region. Even though he had learned the new technology of a modern silk filature, because of the lack of infrastructure networks for any industry in China at that time, he had to improvise and design silk reeling machines of "intermediate" technology. The "intermediate" technology introduced by Qiyuan, together with centralization of labor into a cooperative and concentrated place of production (a factory), were crucial for efficient production of good quality silk that satisfied the demand of foreign nations for export. Within a few years after the founding of Jichanglong, nine other filatures were established in the county and a few more in

Shunde. Despite the setback of having to move his filature temporarily to Macau in 1882 as a result of the Silk Weavers' Riot, proliferation of filatures continued in other parts of the Pearl River Delta unaffected by the government's closure order.

He and his son Puxuan, also invented an inexpensive "bicycle silk reeling machine" which was powered by a foot treadle with added technology to improve the quality of reeled silk good enough for export. Many workshops were set up with 10 to 20 such machines with low capital investment. The Pearl River Delta Region was studded with many such workshops for silk production amid the filatures.

The export of raw silk from filatures on the Pearl River Delta rose from 9,556 *piculs* in 1883 to 36,987 *piculs* in 1910.[1] In 1920, at the peak of the silk industry, the Pearl River Delta Region exported 54,366 *piculs* of raw silk, representing around 48% of all raw silk exported from China.[2]

Aware of the progressive deterioration of the quality of the cocoons and the high prevalence of disease among silkworms, Qiyuan researched silkworm rearing. In 1886, he published the book *Cán sāng pǔ*, which was a manual on mulberry and silkworm cultivation, in very simple language for the farmers. Even though useful, the book did not stop the deteriorating quality of the cocoons and the spread of silkworm disease because of the lack of integration of the industry.

Catalyst of Growth for Other Industries

The expansion of the silk industry stimulated the growth of other industries and trade. Qiyuan indirectly promoted the development of mechanized industry in South China. The modified silk reeling machines that Qiyuan designed for Jichanglong were manufactured and installed by Chen Danpu.[3] As filatures mushroomed, Chan Danpu's business prospered. Chen Danpu's machinery shop was also responsible for the manufacture of the "bicycle silk reeling machines." He and his two sons had since established several machinery shops in the Pearl River Delta Region to handle the machines for the silk industry.[4]

Gradually, different locales became specialized in making different filature equipment: steam engines in Lecong (樂從) in Shunde County, boilers in Guangzhou, and water basins in Shiwan (石灣) in Nanhai County.[5] As filatures and workshops boomed, demand for energy, which was supplied at that time by charcoal, increased, thus fuelling the charcoal-production industry.[6] In addition, fertilizer and foreign gas companies, restaurants, and small hotels thrived in the region.

The finance industry also developed and flourished. Buying mulberry leaves, silkworm eggs, and cocoons required considerable funds. Most buyers borrowed from small, traditional, native Chinese banks. In the early 1920s, when the silk industry was at its peak, these native banks mushroomed in Guangdong, predominantly operated by merchants from the Shunde and Nanhai, counties which received abundant remittances from family members who immigrated overseas.

With the unusual self-sufficiency in terms of financial support from abroad and independence from foreign suppliers for machines, plus equipment for filatures and maintenance, the small-scale silk filatures and workshops boomed in the Pearl River Delta Region.

Economic Consequences

The dramatic growth in Shunde's silk reeling enterprises was unprecedented in the short history of China's modern industry. In less than 50 years, Shunde's silk industry shot up to the top position among Chinese-financed enterprises in Guangdong and China.[7]

Sericulture development was not confined just to the Pearl River Delta, but also included strips along the North River, the West River, the East River, and the province's southern corridor. Many specialized markets such as mulberry leaf markets, egg sheet markets, cocoon markets, as well as the finished product of domestic-reeled raw silk flourished in different parts of the Delta, with Shunde as the regional center. These market towns became prosperous.

During the golden age of the silk industry in the early 1920s, there were 540 native banks in Shunde,[8] and Shunde natives accounted for 52% of their ownership and 55.6% of their capital investment. When Nanhai natives were counted, the two counties accounted for 63% of the ownerships and 68.5% of their investment. Shunde's financial strength supported many businesses in Guangzhou and other towns and villages of the Guangdong province. Shunde's filature production became one of the largest tax sources of the province. In 1909, Shunde generated over $2 million in tax revenue.

For a period of about four to five decades until the late-1920s, the Pearl River Delta Region enjoyed unprecedented prosperity.

A Female Workforce and Social Consequences

When Chen Qiyuan founded Jichanglong, he introduced two new features in the labor market: 1) the employment of a large number of silk reeling workers in a centralized filature workshop; and 2) the introduction of women into a workforce with men under the same roof for the first time. In doing this, he changed the role of women in the Pearl River Delta area forever. For the first time, women entered into a work force alongside men in a centralized workshop. This is against the traditional teaching of the Confucian society that dictates women should remain at home and if they worked, it would be in a domestic setting doing handicraft work.

In the filatures, 95% of the workforce was women, and they worked predominantly in cocoon peeling, silk reeling, re-reeling, packing, and silk-waste preparation, while men as supervisors, foremen, firemen, and machinists. Each filature in Shunde had an average of 464 workers ranging from 300 to 800. Most of the female workers came from local villages or small towns nearby, ranging from 13 to 45 years of age, 20 to 30 being the most common. They worked 10 hours per day and seven days per week, starting from lunar New Year to the middle of December. As there was a large pool of female labor in the villages, wages were low, at an average of about US$0.5 per day. Qiyuan also introduced a number of regulations in Jichanglong which were foreign to workers in China: the adoption of quality control of reeled silk using the denier rating scale; a check-out system for women workers at the end of the day to prevent theft of silk; and a bonus and fine system to ensure the quality of silk produced.[9] All these regulations, unheard of before, were strictly enforced.

Filatures in the Pearl River Delta Region had one other advantage over those in the Yangtze River Delta Region with regard to the supply of labor. In the Pearl River Delta area, there were women who resisted marriage, divided into two categories: *zishunu* (自梳女) or "women who groom their own hair," a sisterhood of those vowing never to marry by going through a ceremony to declare publicly their unmarried status; and *buluoja* (不落家) or "women who left their husband's house soon after the marriage ceremony and returned to their natal families for good." These practices predated the first filature and could be traced as early as the Ming Dynasty. These women rose against the cruelty of the feudal family system,[10] and quite unlike their married sisters, they were fiercely independent and moved around traveling freely. The filatures provided these women with economic independence through labor. On the other hand, the independence and work experience of these women made them readily adaptable to filature work and provided a stable labor force for the filatures. Younger *zishunu* worked in filatures while older ones in mulberry leaf picking and silkworm raising.[11]

The marriage resistance movement was found in many parts of Guangdong, but not in the Shanghai area, making it difficult to recruit a female workforce or keep a stable one in the latter region. One factor that encouraged this movement was the large-scale emigration from southern China during the mid-nineteenth century when the population on the Pearl River Delta had grown so much that it was unable to feed itself. Although the great majority of emigrants were young men, some young women, especially *zishunu* and *buloujia,* also went abroad to work.

In 1925, with the proliferation of the filatures in the Pearl River Delta Region, there were some 170,000 workers employed in the industry, most of whom were women. The wages for women were low and the working conditions atrocious. Women and children, some younger than seven years old, toiled in steam-filled rooms, with inadequate ventilation and high temperatures, causing the atmosphere to become suffocating and filled with the stench of dead cocoons.[12] The women and children were often scalded by boiling water used to loosen the silk threads. No employee welfare institution existed; no formal training programs were provided. In Shanghai, young girls were put to work in miscellaneous menial jobs from which they graduated to the boiling of cocoons. They were trained by older women and learned by working as auxiliary reelers, substituting for regular reelers. From their meager pay, they had to provide themselves food and lodging.[13]

It was not surprising that the filature workers rebelled against their atrocious working conditions and low wages. In 1912, in the early days of the Republic of China when Guangdong was ruled by Dr. Sun Yat-sen's provisional military government, some 5,000 women in Shunde went on strike, protesting mistreatment and payment by depreciated currency. Other protests and strikes in different regions followed. The most serious incident occurred in early 1925 when workers demanded higher wages, the cessation of the practice of body searches, and the elimination of fines for alleged poor productivity. A union was formed by the strikers to demand 40% higher wages and the termination of management harassment. In the end, the women were forced to yield. The filature owners, backed by the military, issued a proclamation forbidding the workers to join the union. The parents or brothers of the violators would be held responsible. As a carrot, they offered a 20% increase in wage. At that time, the country was divided and ruled by warlords. The government of Guangdong had been in the hands of various political fractions since 1912; but in 1925, it was back in the hands of Dr. Sun Yat-sen. The government stepped in to intervene, ordering the filatures to recognize the union, to reinstate dismissed workers, and to reimburse workers for the period when the filatures were closed. A number of strikes occurred until the 1930s when many filatures and workshops were closed due to the decline of the silk industry.[14]

The filatures also changed the pattern of gender division of labor in the silk industry. Before the advent of the filatures, the established pattern of labor was that men were weavers while women were spinners or reelers. The arrangement worked well, and the work of men and women complemented each other. Chen Qiyuan realized that women reelers with home experience needed minimal training to become sophisticated workers in filatures, and the adapted workshops. As a result, in the late 1870s, 90% of the workforce in the filatures was women, and men were not employed in this sector, except for in a few higher-ranking or professional jobs, such as managers or engineers.

The emigration of men also compelled women in the silk-producing region to seek work in the filatures to support themselves and their families. Their earnings, although lower than those of men, were crucial to their own economic independence and added considerably to the household economy of many rural families. The establishment of the first filature gave women financial independence and freed them from the bondage of marriage at the time.

Demise of the Traditional Silk Weaving Industry

While the silk filature and its related industries flourished, the traditional local silk weaving industry declined because of reduced domestic raw silk production from lack of cocoon supply. The competition between the silk filatures and the silk weavers for cocoons was fierce, with the former winning most of the time because they could afford to pay a higher price for the products. The fortunes of weavers waxed and waned inversely with the filature silk export.

The silk weavers' guild thrived in the late Qing Dynasty in the urban centers of Guangzhou and Foshan, and in Nanhai and Panyu (番禺) counties. These guilds also acted as government tax collectors in exchange for monopolistic rights. Traditional silk weaving began to decline in the second half of the nineteenth century, partly due to the diversion of the cocoons to filatures. The Silk Weavers' Riot in 1881 was the conclusion of the weavers' frustration and anger at their loss of their livelihood. The weavers enjoyed a temporary reprieve from the closure of filatures in Nanhai. When the ban on filatures was lifted in 1887, a confrontation between several hundred weavers and filature workers erupted into an armed combat.

By the end of the second decade of the twentieth century, there were workshops in the Pearl River Delta area employing from six to seven to more than 100 workers using the "bicycle silk reeling machines," which were invented by Chen Qiyuan and his son. The increased supply of domestic raw silk relieved the problems for the weavers to a certain extent, but in general, because the filatures always offered a good price, cocoons were still being diverted to the filatures. Moreover, the reeled silk produced by the "bicycle silk reeling machines" was of better quality and more often exported. The deterioration of the traditional silk weaving industry continued. In the beginning of the nineteenth century, there were 17,000 weavers in Foshan, and by the end of the nineteenth century, only 2,000 weavers remained.[15] Heavy taxation on silk added to the difficulties of the weavers. The popularity of Western-style clothing made from foreign cotton and woollens in the era of the Republic of China further reduced the market for domestic silk goods. The arrival in 1915 of electrically-powered weaving accelerated the decay of the traditional weaving industry.[15]

Environmental Pollution

Prior to the emergence of filatures, home silk reeling and small, family handloom weaving workshops predominated in the villages in Nanhai and its neighboring counties. The advent of Jichanglong filature changed the lives of Jiancun forever in many aspects. Although the daily three loud shrieks in the morning from the filature cannot be considered as noise pollution today, they were annoying for most people and particularly for those who were late risers. The huge building with its big chimney, spewing out black smoke, polluted the once clean environment of the countryside. Particulates, sulphur dioxide, and oxides of nitrogen found in the smoke are known to cause cardiorespiratory problems. Carbon monoxide, traces of heavy metals, arsenic, and volatile organic compounds from burning charcoal are now known to be harmful to health. The rivers were contaminated by the discharge of wastes from filatures. The beginning of industrialization in Jiancun and in many other villages on the Pearl River Delta and other silk producing regions brought in the inevitable, undesirable effects of pollution to the air and water.

Land Use for Cash Crops

Traditionally, villages in South China had depended on subsistence agriculture for their livelihood. This is a self-sufficient farming system of most agrarian societies, in which the farmer's output is mainly for family or local consumptions. The farm includes a variety of crops and animals needed by the family to feed themselves. In contrast, commercial farming, also known as cash crop farming, is for profit and generates cash for the farmer's livelihood. It is a venture in which a cash crop or crops are grown and intended to be marketed, a common practice of developed nations rather than developing ones.

Although the Pearl River Delta had been a place for sericulture since the Ming Dynasty, the global demand for more raw silk led to more and more agricultural lands being converted for sericulture purposes. By the 1880s, almost all the land in Shunde County, and one-quarter of all the land in Nanhai County were covered with mulberry tree dike-fish ponds. By 1890s, Dongguan County and Sanshui (三水) County also turned agricultural lands into mulberry plantations and silkworm rearing.[16] The highly diversified agriculture in the region was transformed drastically into an economy of dual product—a specialized path of mulberry-dike-fish ponds. As commercialization prevailed in the Delta region, a large number of people were employed by the filatures. The peasants came to depend more on the silk industry and the market exchanges from market-induced specialization rather than on rice or wheat production.

As in any region that solely relies on one or two cash crops for its economy, the people of Pearl River Delta lost their economic self-sufficiency when cash cropping became heavily dependent on the demands and the vicissitudes of the foreign market. In the late 1920s, reduced world demand, lower price of raw silk, high cost of cocoons, and high taxation reduced the profit margin to zero for many filatures. As business dwindled, the filatures closed rapidly one after another. Many became unemployed and the region suffered greatly economically during the decline of the silk industry in the 1930s. The Japanese invasion of China, the Second World War, and the political events that followed ended the export of silk from China.

In summary, Chen Qiyuan's inventions triggered China's silk industrial revolution in the rural hinterland of Guangzhou. Because of his invention, the Pearl River Delta filature silk accounted for a high proportion of all silk exported from China for more than four decades before the Second World War. His wise decision to establish the filature in his native village of Jiancun with abundant raw materials and accessible market locations along with his local connections were important factors that led to his success.

Instead of reproducing the Western silk reeling machines in his native village which had no infrastructure for industry, he modified and adapted the machine so that it could be built locally and inexpensively and did not require any spare parts or maintenance from expensive foreign firms, making the establishment of filatures more affordable for local entrepreneurs while producing good quality silk for export. His other invention, the "bicycle silk reeling machine," an inexpensive foot-powered machine for home use, also improved the quality of home-reeled silk and prolonged the handicraft industry in domestic settings.

Recognizing the importance of organization and management, he introduced a number of innovations in labor management such as utilizing female labor, women working beside men, a check-out system to avoid embezzlement of silk, and a bonus and fine system to encourage good work practices. He also introduced standardized quality control of silk products using denier measures. He was therefore not just a merchant and a sophisticated entrepreneur, but also a unique technical expert with management skills—a pioneer of modern industry in China.

An abrupt economic change in the existing social structure requires careful planning to avoid unintended consequences, and this planning, of course, did not take place. When Chen Qiyuan established his first silk filature in Jiancun, his only concern was to bring prosperity to his native village and the Pearl River Delta Region, an endeavour in which he had succeeded admirably. Despite the inevitable undesirable effects of industrialization, his bold experiment, in the end, was a success story for China's modern industry. It stimulated the growth of other industries and trade, brought in prosperity to his native village and the Pearl River Delta Region for almost five decades, and gave women the chance of financial independence for the first time in China.

Epilogue

During the period after the Second World War up to the 1970s, Japan was the leading silk producer and exporter in the world. There were hardly any mulberry trees left in the silk-producing regions of China after the Second World War. The epic events in China that followed include the civil war between Guomintang and the Chinese Communist Party (which ended with the founding of the People's Republic of China), the Korean War, the United Nations embargo in the early 1950s, and the fallout of political turmoil in the late 1950s and early 1960s which culminated in the Cultural Revolution between 1966 and 1976; all of these conflicts and developments rendered silk production impossible or profitless. President Nixon's visit to China in 1972 not only re-established a diplomatic relationship between the China and the United States, but also opened up China to world economies. By the late 1970s, the economy as well as the silk industry in China gradually improved. The reforms launched by Deng Xiaoping since 1978 accelerated the growth of industries and trade. Today, China has become the world's largest economy after the United States.

In 2015, China accounted for over 80% of global silk production and over 90% of the world's silk exports, overtaking Japan by a huge margin.[1] Learning from mistakes in the past, local governments have actively encouraged the growth of silk industry by introducing a number of incentives such as land policy exemptions, tax breaks, prioritization, and energy discounts (a company can receive discounts of fees related to water, electricity, and gas upon approval). The government also introduced new facilities that are expected to bring the latest high-end, silk-manufacturing machinery. There has been a gradual shift of raw silk production to inland from the coastal regions because of the high land and labor cost on the east and south coasts. With the help of the government's preferential policies,[2] mulberry tree cultivation and sericulture are now concentrated in the inland areas of Chongqing (Sichuan Province) and Yunnan, where land is plentiful and labor is cheaper, while the Yangtze River Delta Region, with industrialized cities like Shanghai, Wuxi, and Hangzhou, has become the center of processing refined silk goods for export.

The Pearl River Delta Region is now one of the most densely urbanized regions in the world. The region, with its nine largest cities (Dongguan, Foshan, Guangzhou, Huizhou (惠州) Jiangmen (江門), Shenzhen (深圳), Zhaoqing (肇慶), Zhongshan (中山), and Zhuhai (珠海), together with Hong Kong and Macau, is considered as an emerging megacity with an estimated combined population of 120 million in 2010/2011.[3] The Pearl River Delta Region has become the world's workshop and is a major manufacturing base for electronic products such as watches and clocks, toys, garments and textiles, plastic products, and a range of other goods. The products are mostly geared for export. It is one of the most economically dynamic regions of China and is responsible for approximately one-third of China's trade value.[4]

Today Jiancun is not a quiet village anymore but has become one of the many nondescript towns in South China. Although it has been spared from much of the industrial development that has gone on in the Pearl River Delta Region, it has grown into a busy town with lots of restaurants and shops. While the Jishu River continues to meander lazily through the village with no boats in it, the traffic on the highway leading to Jiancun is heavy. Along the highway, one can appreciate the tremendous development where rice fields disappeared and were replaced by modern high-rise buildings and factories.

The descendants of Chen Qiyuan come and go; the Chen Qiyuan Memorial Hall remains. It is not a big museum. One finds it among similar village houses, although it occupies a much bigger area than a village house. Its serenity amid the hustle and bustle of everyday life gently reminds us of the past. It was indeed a wise move to convert the Chen Qiting Ancestral Hall into Chen Qiyuan Memorial Hall to remind us not only of the Qiyuan's contributions to the silk industry and to the economy of the Pearl River Delta Region, but also of his patriotism and philanthropy. His selflessness in sharing his inventions with his fellow countrymen, his steadfastness of purpose, adaptability, perseverance, and generosity should be a shining example for us all to emulate.

Notes

Introduction

1.　　Chen Zuohai (陳作海). *The Turbulent History of the Silk Industry: Chen Qiyuan, a Pioneer in Modern Industry of China* (缫絲風雲錄：記中國近代民族工業先驅陳啟沅), Guangzhou: South China University of Technology Press (廣州：華南理工大學出版社), 2017.
2.　　A one-room Chinese school in the old days.
3.　　*Siheyuan* (四合院) is a historical type of residence that was commonly found throughout China, most famously in Beijing. In English, *siheyuans* are sometimes referred to as Chinese quadrangles.

Chapter 1

1.　　Food and Agriculture Organization of the United Nations, "Silk Reeling and Testing Manual", Rome, 1990. http://www.fao.org/docrep/x2099e/x2099e00.htm. Accessed on 10 October 2017
2.　　Robert Eng, *Economic Imperialism in China. Silk Production and Exports, 1862–1932*, China Research Monograph, Institute of East Asian Studies, (University of California, Berkeley Center for Chinese Studies, 1986), 17–18.
3.　　Ibid., 23, (Unequal treaty and silk export).
4.　　Pébrine, or "pepper disease," is a disease of silkworms, which is caused by protozoan microsporidian parasites, mainly Nosema bombycis and, to a lesser extent, Vairimorpha, Pleistophora and Thelohania species and is transmitted from infected females to progeny in the eggs. It was first recorded if France in 1845 ad then spread to other European countries.

5. Robert Eng, *Economic Imperialism in China. Silk Production and Exports, 1862–1932*, 24–28. (Silk import in the US).

6. Ibid., 28–29. (Reasons for increase in silk export).

7. Wong Chor Yee, "Proto-industrialization and the Silk Industry of the Canton Delta, 1662– 1934", (PhD Thesis, University of Madison–Wisconsin, 1995), 269–270.

8. Gui Zhan et al (桂坫等修), Supplement to Nanhai County Annals (南海縣志), 1910 (宣統二年), no 26, 516. (Development of filatures in Nanhai).

9. Wong Chor Yee, "Proto-industrialization and the Silk Industry of the Canton Delta, 1662–1934", 392–393. (Extensive waterways in Shunde).

10. Robert Eng, *Economic Imperialism in China. Silk Production and Exports, 1862–1932*, 40–41. (Expansion of filatures in Shanghai).

11. Ibid., 45. (Filatures in Jiangnan).

12. Ibid., 79. (Merchants engaged in overseas trade in Shunde).

13. Ibid., 107. (Univoltine or bivoltine silkworms).

14. Ibid., 97. (Expansion of mulberry fields during Tongchi Period).

15. Ibid., 99. (Expansion of mulberry dike-fish ponds Canton delta).

16. Ibid., 91. (Chinese goods in ships carrying foreign flag).

17. Ibid.,121. (Specialization in mulberry leaves production and silkworm rearing).

18. Chen Tianjie (陳天杰), Chen Qiutung (陳秋桐), "The First Steam Filature in Guangdong, Jichanglong and Its Founder Chen Qiyuan" ("廣東第一間蒸氣缫絲繼昌隆及其創辦人陳啟沅"), Edited by Nanhai Political Consultative Committee on the Materials of Chinese History (廣州政協文史資料研究委員會編 ,廣州文史資料), 10th edition, 1987, 35. (Cocoon markets).

19. Robert Eng, *Economic Imperialism in China. Silk Production and Exports, 1862–1932*, 111. (Cocoon brokerages and middlemen).
20. Wong Chor Yee, "Proto-industrialization and the Silk Industry of the Canton Delta, 1662–1934", 302. (Shunde and its twin towns - regional centre for cocoon market).
21. Robert Eng, *Economic Imperialism in China. Silk Production and Exports, 1862–1932*, 111. (Purchase cocoons).
22. Ibid., 125–127. (Silkworm disease in China).
23. Ibid., 128. (Larger quantities of cocoons required to produce the same quantity of silk).
24. Ibid., 111–113. (*Likin* was a Chinese provincial tax levied at many inland stations upon imports or articles in transit, introduced in 1851 and abolished in 1931)
25. Ibid., 110. (Taxes).
26. Ibid., 119. (Taxes and *likins* in the late 1920s).
27. Ibid., 129. (Price of raw silk in mid 1920s).
28. Wong Chor Yee, "Proto-industrialization and the Silk Industry of the Canton Delta, 1662–1934", 342, Table 4.61.

Chapter 2

1. Xu Feng (許鋒), A Commentary on the Life of Chan Qiyuan (陳啟沅評傳), (in press)
2. Chen Ruzhi (陳孺直), A Brief History of Modern Genealogy of the Chen Family (陳氏近代族譜簡略), Unpublished
3. *Cihai* is a large-scale Chinese dictionary and encyclopedia. The Zhonghua Book Company published the first *Cihai* edition in 1938, and the Shanghai Lexicographical Publishing House revised editions in 1979, 1989, 1999, and 2009.
4. Chen Ruzhi, *A Brief History of My Ancestors*, Unpublished

5. Chester Fuson, "The Geography of Kwangtung," *Lingnan Science Journal,* 6 (1928): 24.

6. Wong Chor Yee, "Proto-industrialization and the Silk Industry of the Canton Delta, 1662–1934", 20–22 (Population surge and land-population ratio).

7. Chen Zuohai, The Turbulent History of the Silk Industry: Chen Qiyuan, a Pioneer in Modern Industry of China, 3. (Father "retired" and became a farmer).

8. Chen Qiyuan (陳啟沅). *Can Sang Pu* (蠶桑譜, *On Sericulture*), Guangxi: Guangxi Normal University Press (廣西師范大學出版社), 2015.

9. Menzius Discourse with Prince Teng Wengong (孟子.滕文公上). https://baike.baidu.com/item/孟子·滕文公上. Accessed on 15 October 2017

10. Chen Zuohai, *The Turbulent History of the Silk Industry: Chen Qiyuan, a Pioneer in Modern Industry of China,* 3–4. (Father's teaching on joy of farming).

11. Chinese Imperial Examination. https://en.wikipedia.org/wiki/Imperial_examination.

12. *Qiushuǐ xuan chidu* (秋水軒尺牘) Letters from Autumn Water Retreat, a biography written in the form of letters by the author Xu Jiacun (許葭村) during Qing dynasty and regarded as a classic and a standard text for the imperial examination).

13. Other books not in the Child Examination Curriculum but in higher clasess: *Four Books and Five Classics* (四書五經), which illustrates the core value and belief systems in Confucian thought, and the *Analects of Confucius* (論語), and some other books such as *Various Sages and Hundred Schools of Thought* (諸子百家).

14. Chen Zuohai, *The Turbulent History of the Silk Industry: Chen Qiyuan, a Pioneer in Modern Industry of China,* 3. (Qiyuan failed twice in Child Examination).

15. Chinese Imperial Examination. https://en.wikipedia.org/wiki/Imperial_examination. (Failure rate in the imperial examinations)

16. A pendulum clock is a clock that uses a pendulum, a swinging weight, as its timekeeping element. The advantage of a pendulum for timekeeping is that it is a harmonic oscillator; it swings back and forth in a precise time interval dependent on its length, and resists swinging at other rates. From its invention in 1656 by Christiaan Huygens until the 1930s, the pendulum clock was the world's most precise timekeeper, accounting for its widespread use. Throughout the 18th and 19th centuries pendulum clocks in homes, factories, offices and railroad stations served as primary time standards for scheduling daily life, work shifts, and public transportation, and their greater accuracy allowed the faster pace of life which was necessary for the Industrial Revolution. The home pendulum clock was replaced by cheaper synchronous electric clocks in the 1930s and '40s, and they are now kept mostly for their decorative and antique value. (https://en.wikipedia.org/wiki/Pendulum_clock).

17. "Coastal Border Region and Market" ("海疆與互市"), General History of China (中國通史) CCTV6, Episode 82. (China barricaded itself).

18. "White Silver as Capital" ("白銀資杰"), General History of China (中國通史), CCTV6, Episode 86.

19. The system was highly regulated by the Qing government—foreign traders were only allowed to trade through a body of Chinese merchants known as the Cohong. Foreigners could only live in one of the Thirteen Factories (十三行).

20. "The Opium War" ("鴉片戰争"), General History of China (中國通史), CCTV6, Episode 96.

21. Steve Tsang, *A Modern History of Hong Kong*, (Hong Kong: Hong Kong University Press, 2007), 3–13. (Opium trade, opium war).

22. Ibid., 3–13.

23. The Maritime Customs Service was a Chinese governmental tax collection agency and information service from its founding in 1854 until it split in 1949 into services operating in the Republic of China on Taiwan, and in the People's Republic of China. From its foundation in 1854 until the collapse of the Qing dynasty in 1911, the agency was known as the Imperial Maritime Customs Service. The Salt Adminstration or Salt Industry Commission in China was an organization created in 758, during the decline of Tang dynasty China, used to raise tax revenue from the state monopoly of the salt trade, or salt gabelle. The Commission sold salt to private merchants at a price that included a low but cumulatively substantial tax, which was passed on by the merchants at the point of sale. This basic mechanism of an indirect tax collected by private merchants supervised by government officials endured to the mid-20th century. The salt tax enabled a weak government to sustain itself; the government need control only the few regions that produced salt.

24. Robert Eng, *Economic Imperialism in China. Silk Production and Exports, 1862–1932,* 5. (Treaty of Nanking).

25. William J. Bernstein, *A Splendid Exchange: How Ttade Shaped the World*, (New York: Atlantic Monthly Press. 2008), 286. (Chinese population in 1766–1833).

26. Paul A. Van Dyke, *The Canton Trade: Life and Enterprise on the China Coast, 1700–1845*. (Hong Kong: Hong Kong University Press, 2005), 6–9.

27. "Taiping Rebellion" ("太平天國"), General History of China (中國通史), CCTV6, Episode 97.

28. Chen Zuohai, *The Turbulent History of the Silk Industry: Chen Qiyuan, a Pioneer in Modern Industry of China,* 6. (Qiyuan's toy with the idea of joining Taiping Rebellion).

29. Ibid, 6. (Qiyuan lost his father).

30. Huang Jinkun (黃景坤), "The Life of Chen Qiyuan" ("陳啟沅傳"), Nanhai Political Consultative Committee on the Materials of Chinese History, Materials on History of Nanhai (南海政協文史資料研究委員會編，南海文史資料), 10th edition, 1987, 3.

31. Wu Jianxin (吳建新), *The Life of Chen Qiyuan* (陳啟沅傳), Guangdong: Guangdong People's Publishing House (廣東: 廣東人民出版社), 2012, 2. (Teaching in the si-shu).

32. Chen Zuohai, *The Turbulent History of the Silk Industry: Chen Qiyuan, a Pioneer in Modern Industry of China,* 5. (Sweet Potato Yuan).

33. Ibid., 6. (Qishu went to Annam). Wu Jianxin. *The life of Chen Qiyuan*, 7. (Qishu sent his wife and children to father in law)

34. Ibid., 6. (Qishu returned after 3 years).

35. Ibid., 6–7. (Agreement between the three brothers).

36. Persia C. Campbell. *Chinese Coolie Emigration within the British Empire*. London: P. S. King and Soon ltd., Prichard House, Westminster, 1923, xvii.

37. Ta Chen, "Chinese Emigration". *US Department of Labor Bulletin,* 340 Washington 1923, 17.

38. History of Macau. https://en.wikioedia.org/wiki/History _of_ Macau. (Macau as transit center for coolie trade). Accessed pm 15 October 2017

39. M. Chan-Yeung, *Lam Woo, Master Builder, Revolutionary and Philanthropist,* Hong Kong: Chinese University Press, 2017, 5–9.

40. Chinese junk ship. https://en.wikipedia.org/wiki/Junk _(ship). Accessed on 15 October 2017

41. Chen Zuohai, *The Turbulent History of the Silk Industry: Chen Qiyuan, a Pioneer in Modern Industry of China*. 8–10. (Ship wreck).

Chapter 3

1. Huang Jinkun, "The Life of Chen Qiyuan", 4. (Arrival of the brothers in Annam in 1854).
2. Ky Luong Nhi, "The Chinese in Vietnam. A Study of Vietnamese-Chinese Relation with Special Attention to the Period 1862-1961". PhD thesis, University of Michigan, 1963, 15–26.
3. Ibid., 27–28.
4. Ramses Amer, "The Ethnic Chinese in Vietnam and Sino-Vietnamese Relations", *Forum Kula Lumpur*, (1991), 5–9.
5. The Origin of Cholon (堤岸的源起). http://www.chebamau.com/the-origin-of-cholon.
6. Charles Lemire, Saigon-Cholon in 1868, http://www.historicvietnam.com/Saigon_Cholon_1968/.
7. In 1889, the French had more accurate statistics and found 56,528 Chine living in the whole Cochichina. Of these, 15,000 were living in Cholon and 8,250 in Saigon. (Annuaire Statistique de l'Indochine francaise, Saigon: 1889), 530. Accessed on 24 October 2017
8. Charles Lemire, Saigon-Cholon in 1868, http://www.historicvietnam.com/Saigo_Cholon_1968/, 23. Accessed on 24 October 2017
9. https://baike.baidu.com/item/阿婆廟 Accessed on 24 October 2017
10. Chen Zuohai, *The Turbulent History of the Silk Industry: Chen Qiyuan, a Pioneer in Modern Industry of China*, 11. (Junhezhan Grocery Store).
11. Ibid., 12. (Progress after a few months).

12. Ibid., 12. (Fixing ex-employer's clock).
13. Ibid., 13. (Checked accuracy of the clock).
14. Ibid., 14–15. (Hired assistant to fix clocks and watches).
15. Ibid., 16. (Assessing the business of repair of clocks and watches).
16. Ibid., 16. (Sending money home).
17. Lewis B. Lockwood and Allan K. Smith, Fermented Soy Foods and Sauce. 1950–1951 Yearbook of agriculture. https://naldc.nal.usda.gov/download/IND43894083/PDF Accessed on 5 November 2017
18. Chen Zuohai, *The Turbulent History of the Silk Industry: Chen Qiyuan, a Pioneer in Modern Industry of China*, 17–18. (均和昌醬園).
19. Arrival of Europeans in Vietnam. http://factsanddetails.com/southeast-asia/Vietnam/sub5_9a/entry-3337.html. (France colonizing Vietnam). Accessed on 5 November 2017
20. Ramses Amer, "The Ethnic Chinese in Vietnam and Sino-Vietnamese Relations". 9. (Tax on Chinese).
21. Arrival of Europeans in Vietnam. http://factsanddetails.com/southeast-asia/Vietnam/sub5_9a/entry-3337.html. (The Chinese were involved in many different business in Vietnam). Accessed on 5 November 2017
22. Yuanyuan Pan, Yang Xunan, Xingjuan Chen, Meiying Xu, Guoping Sun, "The right mud: Studies in the mud-coating technique of Gambiered Guangdong silk", *Applied Clay Science*, 135 (2017): 516–520.
23. Chen Zuohai, *The Turbulent History of the Silk Industry: Chen Qiyuan, a Pioneer in Modern Industry of China Chen Qiyuan*, 19. (Zhou Chao business).
24. Huang Jinkun, "The Life of Chen Qiyuan", 5. Chen Zuohai, *The Turbulent History of the Silk Industry: Chen Qiyuan, a Pioneer*

in *Modern Industry of China*, 19. (Various shops of the Chen brother).

25.   History of Pawnbooking http://en.wikipedia.org/wiki/History_of_pawnbroking. Accessed on 26 November 2017

26.   Chen Zuohai, *The Turbulent History of the Silk Industry: Chen Qiyuan, a Pioneer in Modern Industry of China*, 20. (Licence for pawnshop business).

27.   Ibid., 21. (Guidelines for pawnshop).

28.   Yingnan Xu. "Industrialization and the Chinese Hand-reeled Silk Industry, 1880–1930," *Penn History Review*, 19 (2011): 27–45.

29.   Lee Yong-woo, "Silk Reeling and Testing Manual". FAO Agricultural Services Bulletin No 136. Food and Agriculture Organization of the United Nations, (Rome. 1999), http://www.fao.org/docrep/x2099e/x2099e07.htm. Accessed 26 November 2017

30.   Wong Chor Yee, "Proto-industrialization and the Silk Industry of the Canton Delta, 1662- 1934", 277. (Chinese silk export losing ground to Japan).

31.   Chen Zuohai, *The Turbulent History of the Silk Industry: Chen Qiyuan, a Pioneer in Modern Industry of China* 25. (Obtain a loan to buy silk reeling machine from foreign countries).

32.   Ibiid., 21. (Foreign companies refused to sell).

33.   The French Chambon system is sometimes also called the double-twisting system while the Italian Tavelle is referred to as self-twisting. The French Chambon system was limited to the use of only two reels per silk reeling basin. The Tavelle system, an Italian system, had no such restrictions and was more productive than the Chambon system.

34.   Giovanni Federico, *An Economic History of the Silk Industry 1830-1930,* Cambridge, UK: Cambridge University Press, 1997, 3. (Improvement in quality of silk).

35. Debin Ma, "Between Cottage and Factory: The Evolution of Chinese and Japanese Silk reeling Industries in the Latter Half of the Nineteenth Century". *Journal of the Asia Pacific Economy;* 10 (2005):195-213. (mechanization of silk reeling).

36. Chen Zuohai, *The Turbulent History of the Silk Industry: Chen Qiyuan, a Pioneer in Modern Industry of China*, 26. Wu Jianxin, *The Life of Chen Qiyuan*, 12–13. (Learning the technology himself).

37. Chen Zuohai, *The Turbulent History of the Silk Industry: Chen Qiyuan, a Pioneer in Modern Industry of China*, 27. (Qishu's advice).

38. Ibid., 28–29. (Lee designed the curriculum).

39. Huang Jinkun, "The Life of Chen Qiyuan", 5. Debin Ma, "Between Cottage and Factory: The Evolution of Chinese and Japanese Silk reeling Industries in the Latter Half of Nineteenth Century", 203. (Qiyuan visited filatures in Thailand and other places).

40. Lee Yong-woo, "Silk Reeling and Testing Manual", FAO Agricultural Services Bulletin No 136. Food and Agriculture Organization of the United Nations, Rome. 1999. http://www.fao.org/docrep/x2099e/x2099e07.htm, Appendix (Other activities in filature). Accessed on 15 October 2017

41. Chen Zuohai, *The Turbulent History of the Silk Industry: Chen Qiyuan, a Pioneer in Modern Industry of China*, 30–31. (Chinese no basic education on science).

42. He Hualuo (何花落), "In Praise of Chen Qiyuan for Establishing the First Modern Silk reeling Machine in Nanhai" ("贊陳啟沅引進我縣第一套近代機器繰絲設備"), Nanhai Political Consultative Committee on the Materials of Chinese History. Materials on History of Nanhai (南海政協文史資料研究委員會編．南海文史資料), 10th edition, 1987. 68.

43.   Chen Zuohai, *The Turbulent History of the Silk Industry: Chen Qiyuan, a Pioneer in Modern Industry of China)*, 33–34. (Sighting steamship far away).

Chapter 4

1.   Chen Tianjie, Chen Qiutung, "The First Steam Filature in Guangdong, Jichanglong and Its Founder Chen Qiyuan", 27.
2.   Debin Ma, "Between Cottage and Factory: The Evolution of Chinese and Japanese Silk reeling Industries in the Latter Half of the Nineteenth Century", 200–202. Robert Eng. *Economic Imperialism in China. Silk Production and Exports, 1862–1932*, 39. (Ewo Failture in Shanghai).
3.   Wong Chor Yee, "Proto-industrialization and the Silk Industry of the Canton Delta, 1662–1934", 300–302. (Shunde superiority in georgraphy)
4.   Huang Jinkun, "The Life of Chen Qiyuan", 6. Chen Tianjie, Chen Qiutung, "The First Steam Filature in Guangdong, Jichanglong and Its Founder Chen Qiyuan", 28. (Jiancun for building filature).
5.   Chen Tianjie, Chen Qiutung, "The First Steam Filature in Guangdong, Jichanglong and Its Founder Chen Qiyuan", 29. (Purchased lot next to the ancestral home).
6.   Huang Jinkun, "The Life of Chen Qiyuan", 6. (7000 taels of white silver from Annam). Wong Chor Yee. "Proto-industrialization and the Silk Industry of the Canton Delta, 1662–1934," 277. (Who financed the filature)
7.   Robert Eng, *Economic Imperialism in China. Silk Production and Exports, 1862–193*2, 357.
8.   Wong Chor Yee, "Proto-industrialization and the Silk Industry of the Canton Delta, 1662–1934", 309–311. Chen Zuohai, *The Turbulent History of the Silk Industry: Chen Qiyuan, a Pioneer in Modern Industry of China,* 37. (Chen Danpu).

9. Huang Jinkun, "The Life of Chen Qiyuan", 6. He Hualuo, "In Praise of Chen Qiyuan for Establishing the First Modern Silk reeling Machine in Nanhai", 68. (Two teams of men).
10. Debin Ma, "Between Cottage and Factory: The Evolution of Chinese and Japanese Silk reeling Industries in the Latter Half of the Nineteenth Century", 204. (Use chopsticks to remove dirt).
11. Chen Tianjie, Chen Qiutung, "The First Steam Filature in Guangdong, Jichanglong and Its Founder Chen Qiyuan", 30. Chen Zuohai, *The Turbulent History of the Silk Industry: Chen Qiyuan, a Pioneer in Modern Industry of China*, 37. (Staff in filature).
12. Wong Chor Yee, "Proto-industrialization and the Silk Industry of the Canton Delta, 1662–1934", 279–280. Debin Ma, "Between Cottage and Factory: The Evolution of Chinese and Japanese Silk reeling Industries in the Latter Half of the Nineteenth Century", 204. (Chen Danpu's business prosper).
13. Huang Jinkun, "The Life of Chen Qiyuan", 6. Chen Tianjie, Chen Qiutung, "The First Steam Filature in Guangdong, Jichanglong and Its Founder Chen Qiyuan", 29–30. (Jichanglung's equipments)
14. Wong Chor Yee, "Proto-industrialization and the Silk Industry of the Canton Delta, 1662–1934", 274–276. Chen Tianjie, Chen Qiutung, "The First Steam Filature in Guangdong, Jichanglong and Its Founder Chen Qiyuan", 29–30. (Number of basins).
15. Gui Zhan et al., Supplement to Nanhai County Annals, 1910, No. 26, 516–517.
16. Wong Chor Yee, "Proto-industrialization and the Silk Industry of the Canton Delta, 1662–1934", 277. Debin Ma, "Between Cottage and Factory: The Evolution of Chinese and Japanese Silk Reeling Industries in the Latter Half of the Nineteenth Century". 204. Gui Zhan et al., Supplement to Nanhai County Annals, 1910, No 21, 432. (Price of reeled silk from Jiachanglong higher than domestic reeled silk).

17. Wong Chor Yee, "Proto-industrialization and the Silk Industry of the Canton Delta, 1662–1934", 277. Chen Zuohai, *The Turbulent History of the Silk Industry: Chen Qiyuan, a Pioneer in Modern Industry of China,* 47. (Silk for Europe and silk for US).

18. Wong Chor Yee, "Proto-industrialization and the Silk Industry of the Canton Delta, 1662–1934", 281. (Chambon system).

19. Li Yuwei and Li Yijie, "Report on a Steam Filature in Guangdong", *The Lingnan Agricultural Rev.* 3, (1925):126–127. (Defects of silk from improper reeling).

20. Chén Déhuá (陳德華), "Worthwhile research questions of Jichanglong Fialture" ("繼昌隆媒絲廠值得探討的幾個問題"), *Journal of Suzhou University. Social Philosophy Edition* (蘇州大學學報哲學社會版), 1, (2000). (It is not clear when steam-powered was introduced into Jichanglong. Some said that when steam power machines were introduced, the workers did not like them and preferred the foot treadle reeling machines).

21. Wong Chor Yee, "Proto-industrialization and the Silk Industry of the Canton Delta, 1662– 1934", 277. (Fines and bonuses).

22. Chen Tianjie, Chen Qiutung, "The First Steam Filature in Guangdong, Jichanglong and Its Founder Chen Qiyuan", 31. Chen Zuohai, *The Turbulent History of the Silk Industry: Chen Qiyuan, a Pioneer in Modern Industry of China,* 40. (Salary of female workers).

23. Chen Tianjie, Chen Qiutung, "The First Steam Filature in Guangdong, Jichanglong and Its Founder Chen Qiyuan", 31. Chen Zuohai, *The Turbulent History of the Silk Industry: Chen Qiyuan, a Pioneer in Modern Industry of China,* 40. (Fines).

24. Chen Tianjie, Chen Qiutung, "The First Steam Filature in Guangdong, Jichanglong and Its Founder Chen Qiyuan", 31. Chen Zuohai, *The Turbulent History of the Silk Industry: Chen Qiyuan, a Pioneer in Modern Industry of China,* 43. (Absence from work).

25.   Chen Tianjie, Chen Qiutung, "The First Steam Filature in Guangdong, Jichanglong and Its Founder Chen Qiyuan", 31–32. (Get used to the strict routine).

26.   Tao Yingchun (陶迎春), "Chen Qiyuan: Founder of the First Silk Filature in China" ("陳啟沅：我國第一家機器繅絲廠創始人"), *Economic Information Daily* (經濟參考報), 25 July, 2008, 12th Edition.

27.   Chen Zuohai, *The Turbulent History of the Silk Industry: Chen Qiyuan, a Pioneer in Modern Industry of China,* 42. (Packaging of silk for export).

28.   Wang Leishi (王磊石), "The bloody case caused by the steam rewinder in the late Qing Dynasty" ("晚清蒸氣繅絲機引發的血案"), Public Welfare Capitalism (公益資本論), History Review, Official Government WeChat, 7 May 2015.

29.   Chen Tianjie, Chen Qiutung, "The First Steam Filature in Guangdong, Jichanglong and Its Founder Chen Qiyuan", 35. (Supply of cocoons).

30.   Ibid., 35. (Strategies to ensure a good supply of cocoons).

31.   Ibid., 36. Robert Eng. *Economic Imperialism in China. Silk Production and Exports, 1862–1932*, 81–84. (*Sizhuang*).

32.   Robert Eng, *Economic Imperialism in China. Silk Production and Exports, 1862–1932,* 89. (Unequal treaties on silk export).

33.   Chen Zuohai, *The Turbulent History of the Silk Industry: Chen Qiyuan, a Pioneer in Modern Industry of China*, 35. (Older generation opposed to the filatures).

34.   Chen Tianjie, Chen Qiutung, "The First Steam Filature in Guangdong, Jichanglong and Its Founder Chen Qiyuan" 37. (Philanthropic activities).

35.   Wang Leishi, "The bloody case caused by the steam rewinder in the late Qing Dynasty", Official Government WeChat, 7 May 2015. Xu Gengbi (除賡陛),"The Second Report of Xuetang Village Riot" ("學堂鄉滋事情形第二稟"), 不自慊齋漫存

Nanhai Publishing House (南海書館), Volume 6, 25–27. Quoted in Peng Zeyi edited (轉引自彭澤益編), Materials on the History of Modern Handicraft Industry (中國近代手工業史資料), Volume 2, Beijing: Life, Study, New Knowledge Joint Publishing (北京：生活，讀書，新知三聯書店), 1957, 46–47.

36.   Chen Zuohai, *The Turbulent History of the Silk Industry: Chen Qiyuan, a Pioneer in Modern Industry of China*, 43. (Criticism and opposition).

37.   Ibid., 43–44. (Juren brothers).

38.   Chen Qiyuan. *Cán sāng pǔ* (蠶桑譜, *On Sericulture*), 15. (1000 visitors in 3 years).

39.   Chen Zuohai, *The Turbulent History of the Silk Industry: Chen Qiyuan, a Pioneer in Modern Industry of China*, 45. (Qiyuan's diffusion of knowledge).

Chapter 5

1.   Chen Tianjie, Chen Qiutung, "Guangdong First Steam Filature, Jichanglong and its Founder Chen Qiyuan", 35. Chen Zuohai, *The Turbulent History of the Silk Industry: The Story of Chen Qiyuan, a pioneer of modern industry of China*, 67. (Strategies to economically induce more sericulture).

2.   Chen Yongsheng (陳永升), "Chen Qiyuan and Jichanglong: The Dilemma of Overseas Chinese Capital in the Late Qing Dynasty" ("陳啟沅與繼昌隆：晚清華僑資本的困境"), China Federation of Historical Research Institute of Overseas Chinese. International Symposium on Xiqiao Culture in Chinese Civilization (中國僑聯歷史研究所, 中華文明視野下的西樵文化, 國際學術研討會論文集), Guangxi: Guangxi Normal University (廣西師範大學出版社), 2012. 371-383. (Loss of livelihood for the silk weavers).

3.   Wong Chor Yee, "Proto-industrialization and the Silk Industry of the Canton Delta, 1662– 1934", 388. (Jinluntang).

4. Robert Eng, *Economic Imperialism in China. Silk Production and Exports, 1862–1932*, 148. (Guild hall as tax collection centre).

5. Robert Eng, *Economic Imperialism in China. Silk Production and Exports, 1862–1932*, 67. Wu Jianxin, *The Life of Chen Qiyuan*" 44. (Illegal activities of Jinluntang).

6. Chen Zuohai, *The Turbulent History of the Silk Industry: Chen Qiyuan, a Pioneer of Modern Industry of China*, 44-45. (Coexistence of filature and silk weavers).

7. Chen Zuohai, *The Turbulent History of the Silk Industry: Chen Qiyuan, a Pioneer in Modern Industry of China*, 48. (Qiyuan preparing for confrontation).

8. Some people called this "Xuetang Riot of 1881" because it occurred in the village called Xuetang.

9. Gui Zhan et al, Supplement to Nanhai County Annals, no 26, 1910, 56–57. Chen Zhohai. *The Turbulent Stormy History of the Silk Industry: Chen Qiyuan, a Pioneer of Modern Industry of China*, 52. (Poor harvest of cocoons).

10. Chen Zuhoai, *The Turbulent History of the Silk Industry: Chen Qiyuan, a Pioneer in Modern Industry of China*, 53. (Targets of Jinluntang).

11. Xu Gengbi (除賡陛), "The Second Report of Xuetang Village Riot" ("學堂鄉滋事情形第二稟," 不自慊齋漫存, Nanhai Publishing House (南海書館), Volume 6, 21–24. Quoted in Peng Zeyi edited (轉引自彭澤益編), Materials on the History of Modern Handicraft Industry (中國近代手工業史資料), Volume 2, Beijing: Life, Study, New Knowledge Joint Publishing (北京：生活，讀書，新知三聯書店), 1957, 46–47. (The silk weavers' riot)

12. Chen Zuohai, *The Turbulent History of the Silk Industry: Chen Qiyuan, a Pioneer of Modern Industry of China*, 55. (Machines destroyed).

13. Ibid., 55. (Two weavers captured and two drowned).

14. Wang Leishi, "The bloody case caused by the steam rewinder in the late Qing Dynasty", Official Government WeChat, 7 May 2015

15. Chen Zuohai, *The Turbulent History of the Silk Industry: Chen Qiyuan, a Pioneer of Modern Industry of China,* 56. (Guarding Jiancun)

16. Ibid., 56 (Silk weavers refused to leave Jiancun).

17. Huang Jinkun, "Chen Qiyuan", 1987, 10–11.

18. Xu Gengbi (除賡陛), "Closure Orders for Owners of Silk Filatures" ("禁止絲偈，曉渝機工示" 不自慊齋漫存), Nanhai Publishing House (南海書館), Volume 6, 17–18. Quoted in Peng Zeyi edited (轉引自彭澤益編), Materials on the History of Modern Handicraft Industry (中國近代手工業史資料), Volume 2, Beijing: Life, Study, New Knowledge Joint Publishing (北京：生活，讀書，新知三聯書店), 1957, 48.

19. Chen Zuohai, *TheTurbulent Stormy History of the Silk Industry*: *Chen Qiyuan, a Pioneer of Modern Industry of China,* 58. (Two companies of soldiers from the Governor).

20. Huang Jinkun, "The Life of Chen Qiyuan", 9. Chen Zhohai, *The Turbulent History of the Silk Industry: Chen Qiyuan, a Pioneer of Modern Industry of China,* 59. (Continuous conflict).

21. Xu Gengbi, "Closure Orders for Owners of Silk Filatures", Nanhai Publishing House , Volume 6, 17–18.

22. Huang Jinkun, "The Life of Chen Qiyuan", 9. Chen Zhohai, *The Turbulent History of the Silk Industry: Chen Qiyuan, a Pioneer of Modern Industry of China*, 59. (Weavers refused to leave the temple).

23. Huang Jinkun, "The Life of Chen Qiyuan", 10; Chen Zhohai, *The Stormy History of the Silk Industry: Chen Qiyuan, a Pioneer of Modern Industry of China*, 60. (Arrival of three companies of soldiers).

24. "On Using Machines to Reel Silk" ("機器繅絲說"), *Shenbao*, no 3151, 5 February, 1882, I. "After Reading the

Discourse on Machine Rreeled Silk" ("閱西友論繅絲局書後"), *Shenbao* No 3443, November 30, 1882, I.

25.   "On Using Machines to Reel Silk Again" ("再論機器繅絲"), *Shenbao*, no 3446, 3 December, 1882, I.

26.   Robert Eng, *Economic Imperialism in China. Silk Production and Exports, 1862–1932, 92.* (Self-strengthening movement and private enterprise).

27.   Same as Note 18. Xu Gengbi, "Closure Orders for Owners of Silk Filatures", Nanhai Publishing House , Volume 6, 17–18.

28.   Huang Jinkun, "The Life of Chen Qiyuan", 11; Chen Tianjie, Chen Qiutung, "Guangdong First Steam Filature, Jichanglong and its Founder Chen Qiyuan", 70. (Move to Macau).

29.   Li Guorong, Chief editor (李國榮主編), Tan Bo, Li Bing (覃波, 李炳編著), "The Secrets of foreign businessmen in the Qing Dynasty (清朝洋商秘檔) https://books.google.com.hk/books?isbn=9575630297 Accessed on 16 December 2017

30.   History of Macau. https://en.wikipedia.org/wiki/History_of_Macau. Accessed on 16 December 2017

31.   Lin Guangzhi (林廣志), Lu Zhipeng (呂志鵬), "The Rise of Chinese Merchants in Macau in Recent Years and Their Contributions to Modern History—With Focus on the Family of Lu Jiu" ("澳門近代華商的崛起及其歷史頁獻—盧九家經為中心"), South China. *Journal of South China Normal University. Social Science Edition* (華南師范大學學報．社會料學版), 1 (2011), 45.

32.   Chen Tianjie, Chen Qiutung, "Guangdong First Steam Filature, Jichanglong and its Founder Chen Qiyuan", 39. (women workers from Jiancun and nieghbour villages).

33.   There is another version of the story of Qiyuan in Macau. According to Xu Feng (許峰) the name Hechang filature could not be found in the Macau Government Gazette of that period. Instead, a filature by the name of Yuehechang (粵和昌), a name used by enterprises operated under He Lianwang, was registered

at the same address as Hechang. It was more than likely that the filature of Qiyuan was registered as Yuehechang, the official name of He Lianwang's enterprises.

34. Huang Jinkun, "The Life of Chen Qiyuan", 11. Chen Tianjie, Chen Qiutung, "Guangdong First Steam Filature, Jichanglong and its Founder Chen Qiyuan", 71 (Hechang- name of filature).

35. Tang Kaijian（湯開建）, "The Family Affairs of He Lianwang, a Highly Successful Businessman of Macau in the Late Qing Dynasty"("晚清澳門華人巨商何連旺考述"), *Modern Chinese History Studies* (近代史研), 1 (2013), 79.

36. Wu Jianxin (吴建新), *The Life of Chén Qǐyuán* (陳啟沅傳), Guangdong: Guangdong People's Publishing House (廣東：廣東人民出版社), 2012, 48. (Shares given to Lu Jiu and He)

37. Xu Feng, *A Critical Review of the Life of Chan Qiyuan*, in press (New filature in 1891).

38. Lin Guangzhi and Lu Zhipeng,"The Rise of Chinese Merchants in Macau in Recent Years and Their Contributions to Modern History—With Focus on the Family of Lu Jiu", *Journal of South China Normal University. Social Science Edition*. 1 (2011), 45. .

39. From Mencius 語出《孟子》離婁上（十七）淳于髡曰：「男女授受不親，禮與？」 孟子曰：「禮也。」 曰：「嫂溺，則援之以手乎？」 曰：「嫂溺不援，是豺狼也。男女授受不親，禮也；嫂溺援之以手者，權也。」 曰：「今天下溺矣，夫子之不援，何也？」 曰：「天下溺，援之以道；嫂溺，援之以手。子欲手援天下乎？」www.nani.com.tw/slearn/slchin/chin_c/chin_c_b/ chin_c_b7_3.htm. Accessed on 8 January 2018

40. Chen Zuohai, *The Turbulent History of the Silk Industry: Chen Qiyuan, a Pioneer in Modern Industry of China*, 71–74. (Bicycle silk reeling machine).

41.   Huang Jinkun, "The Life of Chen Qiyuan", 10–11; (bicycle reeling machine).
42.   Xu Xinwu ed. (徐新吾主編), *Modern History of Chinese Silk Reeling Industry* (中國近代繅絲工業史), Shanghai: Shanghai People's Publishing House (上海：上海人民出版社), 1990, 126.
43.   Chen Zuohai, *The Turbulent History of the Silk Industry: Chen Qiyuan,a Pioneer in Modern Industry of China*, 75. (Filature using bicycle reeling machine).
44.   Ibid., 76 (Moving back to Jaincun).
45.   Xu Xinwu, *Modern History of Chinese Silk reeling Industry*. Shanghai: Shanghai People's Publishing House. 1990, 117.
46.   Huang Jinkun, "The Life of Chen Qiyuan", 12. (Sichanglun).

Chapter 6

1.   Chen Ruzhi, *A Brief History of My Ancestors* (Unpublished).
2.   Chen Zuohai, *The Turbulent History of the Silk Industry: Chen Qiyuan, a Pioneer in Modern Industry of China*, 84–86. (The building of Baiyufang and division of assets among the brothers' families).
3.   Ibid., 86–88. As above.
4.   Chen Tianjie, Chen Qiutung, "The First Steam Filature in Guangdong, Jichanglong and Its Founder Chen Qiyuan", 32. (Rice store etc).
5.   Chen Tianjie, Chen Qiutung, "The First Steam Filature in Guangdong, Jichanglong and Its Founder Chen Qiyuan", 37. Chen Zuohai, *The Turbulent History of the Silk Industry: Chen Qiyuan, a Pioneer in Modern Industry of China*, 107. (Free medicine and burial).

6. Chen Zuohai, *The Turbulent History of the Silk Industry: Chen Qiyuan, a Pioneer in Modern Industry of China*, 105–106. (Free Education).

7. Xu Feng, *A Commentary on the Life of Chan Qiyuan*, (in press) (Simple accounting).

8. Chen Zuohai, *The Turbulent History of the Silk Industry: Chen Qiyuan, a Pioneer in Modern Industry of China,* 105. (Repair mulberry dikes).

9. Ibid., 105. (Repair dikes).

10. Xu Feng, *A Commentary on the Life of Chan Qiyuan,* (in press) (Villagers response).

11. It was not uncommon in those days for the dead to be just dumped on the streets or for the very sick to be left on the streets to die if they had no relatives or friends

12. Charity Halls in Guangzhou in the late Qing dynasty and early Republic of China (清末民初廣州各大善堂概況-廣州文史), www.gzzxws.gov.cn/gzws/cg/cgml/cg9/200808/t20080826/3935.htm. Li Yulin (黎宇琳), "A Brief History of Public Welfare in Guangzhou: From Merchants and Charity Halls to Charity Domain of Common Governance of Officials and People" ("廣州公益簡史：從商紳善堂到 '官民共治' 的慈善之域"), *China Philanthropy Times* (公益時報), April 2017, 16th Edition.

13. Li Yulin, "A Brief History of Public Welfare in Guangzhou: From Merchants and Charity Halls to Charity Domain of Common Governance of Officials and People", *China Philanthropy Times,* April 2017, 16th Edition.

14. Chen Zuohai, *The Turbulent History of the Silk Industry: Chen Qiyuan, a Pioneer in Modern Industry of China*, 106 (Unwanted children).

15. Xu Feng, *A Commentary on the Life of Chan Qiyuan*, (in press). (4th Clinic).

16. Gui Zhan et al., Supplement to Nanhai County Annals, 1910, no 21, 4–6. (Charity halls).

17.　Chen Qiyuan, *Cán sāng pǔ* (蠶桑譜, *On Sericulture*) Guangxi: Guangxi Normal University Press (廣西師范大學出版社), 2015

18.　Huang Jinkun, "The Life of Chen Qiyuan", 15. Wu Jianxin, *The Life of Chen Qiyuan*, 70.

19.　Wu Feng (吳對), *Foreword to Cán sāng pǔ* (蠶桑譜, *On Sericulture*). Guangdong Nanhai Political Consultative Committee on the Materials of Chinese History. Materials on History of Nanhai Can Sang Pu Special Edition (廣東省南海市政協文史資料委員會編蠶桑譜專輯), April, 1994, 5.

20.　Wu Jianxin, *The Life of Chen Qiyuan*, 74. (Four editions of the sericulture book).

21.　Gou Tiejun (苟鐵軍), *Commentary. On Sericulture* (評介．蠶桑譜), Guangxi Normal University Press (廣西師範大學出版社), 2015. 8.

22.　Wu Jianxin, *The Life of Chen Qiyuan*, 75. (Specialist of sericulture).

23.　Xu Feng, *A Commentary on the Life of Chan Qiyuan*, (in press). (Wide distribution of the book in Guangdong).

24.　Chen Qiyuan (陳啟沅). *Chen Qiyuan Mathematics* (陳啟沅算學), Guangxi: Guangxi Normal University Press (廣西桂林，廣西師范大學出版), 2015.

25.　Xu Feng, *A Commentary on the Life of Chan Qiyuan*, (in press). (Publication of the mathematics book).

26.　Chen Zuohai, *The Turbulent History of the Silk Industry: Chen Qiyuan, a Pioneer in Modern Industry of China*, 122–123. (Qiyuan's other books).

27.　Huang Jinkun, "The Life of Chen Qiyuan", 15-16. (Study of other philosophers).

28.　Ibid., 16. Gui Zhan et al., Supplement to Nanhai County Annals, 1910, no 21, 432. Zheng Rong et al in the Qing Dynasty (清鄭荣等修), "The Life of Chen Qiyuan" ("陳啟沅列傳"), Supplement to Nanhai County Annals (南海縣志), Taipei. Cheng

Wen Publishing Company (臺北：成文出版社有限公司), 1947, Volume 4, 1729. (Unusual gift).

29.   Kangxi Dictionary was the standard Chinese dictionary during the 18th and 19th centuries. The Kangxi Emperor of the Manchu Qing Dynasty ordered its compilation in 1710. The dictionary contains more than 47,000 characters, though some 40% of them are graphic variants. In addition, there are rare or archaic characters, some of which are attested only once. Less than a quarter of these characters are now in common use.

30.   Chen Zuohai, *The Turbulent History of the Silk Industry: Chen Qiyuan, a Pioneer in Modern Industry of China*, 90. (Microscript).

31.   Huang Jinkun, "The Life of Chen Qiyuan", 16. (Gift to Chongqi).

32.   Chen Zuohai, *The Turbulent History of the Silk Industry: Chen Qiyuan, a Pioneer in Modern Industry of China,* 90–91.

33.   Ibid., 90. (Others who could microscript).

34.   Ibid., 91. (Rat hair used for microscript).

35.   Tao Mo (陶模) was born in Zhejiang, became Jinshi (進士) in the Imperial Examination system in Tongzhi 7 years. He became governor (巡撫) of Xinjiang in Guāngxù (光绪) 17 years, governor of Shaanxi and Gansu in Guāngxù 21st year; and governor of Guangxi and Guangdong in Guāngxù 26th year. He died in Guāngxù 28th year, two years later. He was an important official of the Qing dynasty because of his support for reform and to learn western methods in science and technology.

36.   Huang Jinkun, "The Life of Chen Qiyuan", 17. (Mining rights dispute).

37.   Chen Zuohai, *The Turbulent History of the Silk Industry: Chen Qiyuan, a Pioneer in Modern Industry of China*, 93–94. (Invitation to do surveying).

38.   Ibid., 96. (Marking property lines).

39.   Ibid., 97. (Hon official title).

40. Ibid., 98. (Gift to Chong Qi).
41. Shortly after in 1900, Chong Qi killed himself after he lost his whole family when Beijing was invaded by the Army of Eight Nations and the Summer Palace was burnt.
42. Chen Zuohai, *The Turbulent History of the Silk Industry: Chen Qiyuan, a Pioneer in Modern Industry of China*, 99. (Chong qi's poem).
43. Ibid., 101. (Five years mining licence).
44. Ibid., 101–102. (Gold mine in Tibet).
45. Chen Ruzhi, *A Brief History of My Ancestors*, Unpublished. (There is a dscrepancy in the year of death according to different sources. According to family records, it should be in 1906).

Chapter 7

1. Data displayed in the exhibit in Chen Qiyuan Memorial Hall. Wong Chor Yee. "Proto-industrialization and the Silk Industry of the Canton Delta, 1662–1934", 183 (Filature silk replacing hand-reeled silk in export).
2. Lillian M. Li, *China's Silk Trade: Traditional Industry in the Modern World 1842–1937*. Mass.: Harvard University Press, 1981, 78.
3. Wong Chor Yee, "Proto-industrialization and the Silk Industry of the Canton Delta, 1662–1934", 311. (Fialture equipment fabricated locally).
4. Wu Jianxin, *The life of Chen Qiyuan*, 20–2. (Machines produced by Chan Danpu and his sons).
5. Wong Chor Yee, "Proto-industrialization and the Silk Industry of the Canton Delta, 1662-–1934, 51. (Proliferatoin of other industries).
6. Ibid., 334. (Charcoal production).
7. Ibid., 326. (Shunde finaical center)).

8.   Ibid., 305. (Money shops in Shunde).
9.   Ibid., 324–325. (System of bonus and fines).
10.   *Zishunu* and *buluojia*. http://www.hxlsw.com/history/qing/zt/2011/1019/66531_2.html. Accessed pn 3 Febraury 2018
11.   Robert Eng, *Economic Imperialism in China. Silk Production and Exports, 1862–1932,* 61–62 (Different work in sericulture for women of different ages).
12.   Gertrude Binder, "Life in Shanghai's Silk Filatures", *The China Weekly Review* (1923–1950) April 6, 1929, ProQuest Hstorical Newspapers: Chinese Newspaper Collection, 231.
13.   Robert Eng, *Economic Imperialism in China. Silk Production and Exports, 1862–1932,* 63. (No formal training for girls and women).
14.   Wang Jingyu (汪敬虞), "Worthwhile Research Questions Related to the Some History of Jiachanglong Silk Filature" ("關于繼昌隆繅絲廠的若干史料及值得研究的幾個問題"), Nanhai Political Consultative Committee on the Materials of Chinese History. Materials on History of Nanhai (南海政協文史資料研究委員會編，南海文史資料), 10th edition, 1987, 59. Robert Eng. Economic Imperialism in China. Silk Production and Exports, 1862–1932, 66–67. (Strike by women workers).
15.   Robert Eng, *Economic Imperialism in China. Silk Production and Exports, 1862–1932,* 131. (Gradual demise of the silk weavers' industry).
16.   Ibid., 99. (Expansion in Canton delta).

Epilogue

1.   International Silk Commission, Statistics http://Inserco.org/en/statistics. Accessed on 3 Febraury 2018
2.   https://en.wikipedia.org/wiki/Silk_industry_in_China. Accessed on 3 Febraury 2018

3. State of the World Cities Report 2010/2011, The United Nations Human Settlements Programme. https://africacheck. org/wp-content/uploads/2014/03/State-of-the-world-cities-2010 .pdf. Accessed on 6 March 2018
4. https://en.wikipedia.org/wiki/Pearl_River_Delta. Accessed on 6 March 2018

Appendix 1: Life Events of Chen Qiyuan

Year	Life Events of Chen Qiyuan	Events in China and Vietnam
1836	Born in Jiancun, Xiqiao, Nanhai	
1839		Beginning of First Opium War
1842		Cession of Hong Kong, opening of 5 treaty ports, and extraterritorial rights to Britain
1850		Beginning of Taiping rebellion
1851	Father died. Assisted teaching *in si-shu* Qishi left for Cholon, Annam	
1854	Married and left with Qishu to Cholon	
1855	Birth of Chan (嬋) first daughter	
1855-1872	Engaged in various businesses in Cholon	
1856		Second Opium War; Britain and France defeated China; more treaty ports opened;
1859		France captured Saigon

1860	Birth of Dafang (達芳), first son (second-born)	Kowloon ceded to Britain as a result of Second Opium War; Self-Strengthening Movement began
1862		France acquired three eastern provinces of Cochinchina
1863	Birth of Puxuan (蒲軒), second son (third-born)	Cambodia became a protectorate of France
1865–1872	Learned about silk reeling machine in Annam	
1970	Birth of Jinyun (錦篔), third son (fifth-born)	
1872	Returned to native village; toured lower Yangtse River Delta Region; began building silk filature in Jiancun	
1873	Jichanglong (繼昌隆) opened	
1875	Birth of Jinzan (錦簪), fourth son (sixth-born)	
1881	Nanhai silk weavers' riots; Jichanglong closed by the local government	
1882	Filature moved to Macau, renamed Hechang (和昌)	
1884	Married 4th wife	
1885	Hechang moved back to Jiancun, renamed Sichanglong (世昌綸)	Sino-French War. France became the protector of Vietnam
1886	Published *Can Sang Pu* (蠶桑譜, *On Sericulture*)	

1886-1890	Puxuan designed bicycle silk reeling machine; Baiyufang (百豫坊) and the ancestral hall built; distribution of estate. Exact year not known	
1887		French Indochina Union formed with Cambodia and Cochinchina, Annam and Tonkin
1889	Published *Chen Qiyuan Suan Xue* (陳啟沅算學 *Chen Qiyuan's Mathematics*)	
1890	Birth of the Ruzhi (孺直) fifth son (ninth-born)	
1893		Laos included in French Indochina Union
1894		Sino-Japanese war began; Revived China Society formed by Sun Yat-sen
1898		Hundred Days Reform in China
1900	Surveying in Shaoquan to resolve mining dispute	Boxer Rebellion— Summer Palace burnt by Army of Eight-Nation Alliance
1904	Qiyuan died in native village	
1911		Xinhai Revolution Establishment of the Republic of China
1928	Jichanglong closed	

227

Footnote: There is no family record on the dates of marriage of Chen Qiyuan to his second and third wife and the dates of birth of his daughters, except for the first one.

Appendix 2: Bibliography

Books and Articles

Amer, Ramses, "The Ethnic Chinese in Vietnam and Sino-Vietnamese Relations." Forum Kula Lumpur, 1991.

Bell, Lynda S. "For Better, For Worse. Women and the World Market in Rural China". *Modern China,* 20 (1994):180–210.

Cameron, M. E. *The Reform Movement in China 1898-1912*. Stanford, California: Stanford University Press, 1931.

Chén Déhuá (陳德華). "繼昌隆繰絲廠值得探討的幾個問題 ("Worthwhile research questions on Jichanglong Filature"), 蘇州大學學報哲學社會版 (*Journal of Suzhou University. Social Philosophy Edition*), 1 (2000).

Chen Qiyuan (陳啟沅). *Cán sāng pǔ* (蠶桑譜, *On Sericulture*), 廣西師范大學出版社 (Guangxi: Guangxi Normal University Press), 2015.

Chen Qiyuan (陳啟沅). *Chen Qiyuan Suan Xue* (陳啟沅算學, *Chen Qiyuan's Book of Mathematics*), 廣西師范大學出版社 (Guangxi: Guangxi Normal University Press), 2015.

Chen Ruzhi (陳孺直), 家中先人事略 (*A Brief History of My Ancestors*) Unpublished.

Chen Ruzhi (陳孺直), 本人大事記 (*Important Events of My Life*) Unpublished.

Chen Ruzhi (陳孺直), 陳氏近代族譜簡略 (A *Brief History of Modern Genealogy of the Chen Family*) Unpublished.

Chen Tianjie (陳天杰), Chen Qiutung (陳秋桐), 廣東第一間蒸氣繅絲繼昌隆及其創辦人陳啟沅 (The First Steam Filature in Guangdong, Jichanglong and Its Founder Chen Qiyuan"), 廣州政協文史資料研究委員會編, 廣州文史資料, (edited by Nanhai Political Consultative Committee on the Materials of Chinese History), 10th edition, 1987.

Chan, Wellington K. K. *Merchants, Mandarins and Modern Enterprises in Late Ching China.* Cambridge: Harvard University East Asian Research Centre, 1977.

Chen Yongsheng (陳永升), 陳啟沅與繼昌隆:晚清華僑資本的困境 (Chen Qiyuan and Jichanglong: The Dilemma of Overseas Chinese Capital in the Late Qing Dynasty). 中國僑聯歷史研究所. 中華文明視野下的西樵文化, 國際學術研討會論文集 (China Federation of Historical Research Institute of Overseas Chinese. International Symposium on Xiqiao Culture in Chinese Civilization), 廣西師范大學出版社 (Guangxi: Guangxi Normal University), 2012.

Chen Zuohai (陳作海). 繅絲風雲錄: 記中國近代民族工業先驅陳啟沅 (*The Turbulent History of the Silk Industry: Chen Qiyuan, a Pioneer in Modern Industry of China*), 廣州: 華南理工大學出版社 (Guangzhou: South China University of Technology Press), 2017.

Chinese Maritime Customs Project, List of Chinese Customs Publications 1940, The Maritime Customs, Documents Illustrative of the Origin, Development, and Activities of the Chinese Customs Services, Volume VII. Shanghai: Statistical Department, Inspectorate General of Customs, 1940.

Edwards, E. W., *British Diplomacy and Finance in China 1895–1914*. Oxford: Claredon Press, 1987.

Eng, Robert Y., *Economic Imperialism in China. Silk Production and Exports 1861–1932*, Institute of East Asian Studies, University of California, Berkeley Centre for Chinese Studies. China Research Monograph, 1986.

Food and Agriculture Organization of the United Nations. "Silk Reeling and Testing Manual", Rome, 1990. http://www.fao.org/docrep/x2099e/x2099e00.htm.

Giovanni, Federico, *An Economic History of the Silk Industry 1830–1930*. Published by EH.NET, December 1997.

Gui Zhan et al. (桂坫等修), 續修南海縣志 (Supplement to Nanhai County Annals), 宣統二年 (1910), 卷 21.

He Hualuo (何花落), 贊陳啟沅引進我縣第一套近代機器繅絲設備 (In Praise of Chen Qiyuan for Establishing the First Modern Silk reeling Machine in Nanhai), 南海政協文央資料研究委員會編, 南海文史資科 (Nanhai Political Consultative Committee on the Materials of Chinese History. Materials on History of Nanhai), 10th edition, 1987.

Huang Jinkun (黃景坤), 陳啟沅傳 (The Life of Chen Qiyuan), 南海政協文史資料研究委員會編. 南海文史資料 (Nanhai Political Consultative Committee on the Materials of Chinese History. Materials on History of Nanhai), 10th edition, 1987.

Lee Yok-shiu, F. Mulberry Dyke-Fish Pond Models, China: A Sustainable Traditional Method of Land-water Ecosystem. Asia-Pacific Environmental Innovation Strategies (APEIS) Research on Innovative and Strategic Policy Options (RISPO) Good Practices Inventory. https://enviroscope.iges.or.jp/contents/APEIS/RISPO/inventory/db/pdf/0152.pdf

Li Lillian M. *China's Silk Trade: Traditional Industry in the Modern World 1842–1837.* Council on East Asian Studies, Harvard University, Cambridge, Mass and London: Harvard University Press, 1981.

Li Lillian M. "Silks by Sea: Trade, Technology, and Enterprise in China and Japan". *Business History Review,* LVI (2), (1982): 192–217.

Li Yulin (黎宇琳), "廣州公益簡史：從商紳善堂到 '官民共治' 的慈善之域" ("A Brief History of Public Welfare in Guangzhou: From Merchants and Charity Halls to Charity Domain of Common Governance of Officials and People"), 公益時報 (*China Philanthropy Times*), April 2017, 16th Edition.

Lin Guangzhi (林廣志), Lu Zhipeng (呂志鵬), "澳門近代華商的崛起及其歷史頁献一盧九家經為中心" ("The Rise of Chinese Merchants in Macau in Recent Years and Their Contributions to Modern History—With Focus on the Family of Lu Jiu"), 華南師范大學學報 社會料學版 (*South China. Journal of South China Normal University. Social Science Edition*). 1 (2011), 45.

Luung, K. Y. "The Chinese in Vietnam: A study of Vietnamese-Chinese Relations with Special Attention to the Period 1862-1961". PhD Thesis, The University of Michigan 1963, Political Science, International Law and Relations, Ann Arbor, Michigan.

Ma, Debin. "Between Cottage and Factory: The evolution of Chinese and Japanese Silk Reeling Industries in the Latter Half of the Nineteenth Century". *Journal of the Asia Pacific Economy;* 10 (2) (2005):195-213.

Macau Gazette (澳門憲報), 8 July 1882, no 4.

Qu Conggui (曲從規), 陳啟沅與中國這代機器繅絲業 (Chen Qiyuan and Chinese History of Silk Reeling Machine Industry), 南海政協文史資料研究委員會編, 南海文史資料 (Nanhai Political Consultative Committee on the Materials of Chinese History. Materials on History of Nanhai), 10th edition, 1987.

Sinn, E., "Emigration from Hong Kong before 1941: General Trends", In: Skeldon R. *Emigration from Hong Kong.* Hong Kong: The Chinese University Press, 1995.

Sinn, E., "Emigration from Hong Kong before 1941: Organization and Impact", In: Skeldon R. *Emigration from Hong Kong.* Hong Kong: The Chinese University Press, 1995.

Skeldon, R. (ed). *Emigration from Hong Kong.* Hong Kong: The Chinese University Press, 1995.

Sun Yujie (孫玉杰). "近代民族企業中的官商關系探" ("Analysis of the Relationship between Officials and Business in the Modern History of National Entrepreneurship"), 雲南財貿學院學報, 社會料學版 (*Journal of Yunnan University of Finance and Economics, Social Science Edition*), 4 (2006):72.

Tang Kaijian (湯開建), "晚清澳門華人巨商何連旺考述" (The Family Affairs of He Lianwang, a Highly Successful

Businessman of Macau in the Late Qing Dynasty"). 近代史研 (*Modern Chinese History Studies*), 1 (2013), 79.

Tao Yingchun (陶迎春), "陳啟沅： 我國第一家機器繅絲廠創始人" ("Chen Qiyuan: Founder of the First Silk Filature in China"), 經濟參考報 (*Economic Information Daily*), 25 July, 2008, 12th Edition.

Tsin Michael, *Nation, Governance, and Modernity in China. Canton 1900-1927*. Stanford: Stanford University Press, 1999.

Wang Gungwu, *The Chinese Overseas. From Earthbound China to the Quest for Autonomy*. Cambridge, Mass: Harvard University Press, 2000.

Wang Jingyu (汪敬虞), 關于繼昌隆繅絲廠的若干史料及值得研究的幾个問題 (Worth while Research Questions Related to the Some History of Jiachanglong Silk Filature), 南海政協文史資料研究委員會編 南海文史資料 (Nanhai Political Consultative Committee on the Materials of Chinese History. Materials on History of Nanhai), 10th edition, 1987, 59.

Wang Leishi (王磊石). 晚清蒸氣繅絲機引發的血案 (The bloody case caused by the steam rewinder in the late Qing Dynasty), 公益資本論 (Public Welfare Capitalism) History Review, Official Government WeChat, 7 May 2015.

Wong Chor Yee, "Proto-industrialization and the Silk Industry of the Canton Delta, 1662–1934", PhD Thesis, University of Madison–Wisconsin, 1995.

Wu Jianxin (吳建新), 陳啟沅傳 (*The Life of Chén Qǐyuán*), 廣東： 廣東人民出版社, Guangdong: Guangdong People's Publishing House, 2012.

Xu Feng (許鋒), 陳啟沅評傳 (*A Commentary on the Life of Chan Qiyuan*), (in press).

Xu Xinwu (徐新吾), 中國近代繅絲工業史 (*Modern History of Chinese Silk reeling Industry*) 上海：上海人民出版社 (Shanghai: Shanghai People's Publishing House), 1990.

Xu Gengbi (除賡陛), 學堂鄉滋事情形第二稟 (The Second Report of Xuetang Village Riot) in 不自慊齋漫存，南海書館, (Nanhai Publishing House). Volume 6, 21–24. 轉引自彭澤益編 (Quoted in Peng Zeyi edited), 中國近代手工業史資料 (Materials on the History of Modern Handicraft Industry), Volume 2, 北京： 生活， 讀書， 新知三聯書店 (Beijing: Life, Study, New Knowledge Joint Publishing), 1957, 46–47.

Xu Gengbi (除賡陛), 禁止絲偈， 曉渝機工示 (Closure Orders for Owners of Silk Filatures) in 不自慊齋漫存，南海書館 (Nanhai Publishing House) Volume 6, 17–18. 轉引自彭澤益編 (Quoted in Peng Zeyi edited), 中國近代手工

業史資料 (Materials on the History of Modern Handicraft Industry). Volume 2, 北京：生活，讀書，新知三聯書店 (Beijing: Life, Study, New Knowledge Joint Publishing), 1957, 48.

Xu Yingnan. "Industrialization and the Chinese Hand-Reeled Silk Industry (1880-1030)". *Penn History Review,* 19 (1) (2011):26–45

Yen Ching-Hwang. *Ethnic Chinese Business in Asia. History, Culture and Business Enterprise*. Singapore: World Scientific, 2013.

Zheng Rong et al in the Qing Dynasty (清鄭荣等修). 陳啟沅列傳 (*The Life of Chen Qiyuan*) 南海縣志 (Supplement to Nanhai County Annals, 4) 臺北：成文出版社有限公司 (Taipei. Cheng Wen Publishing Company), 1947, 1729.

汪敬虞．從中國生絲對外貿易的變遷看繰絲業資本主義的產生和發展，中國經濟史研究．2001年 第二版．

汪敬虞．十九世紀西方資本主義對中國的經濟浸略，北京：人民出版社，1985年．

汪敬虞主編，中國近代經濟史 (1895-1927)，下冊．北京：人民出版社，2000年．

徐善福，林明華：越南華僑史．東南亞華僑史叢書，朱杰勤主編，廣州廣東高等教育出版社，2011．

黃景坤，關于陳启沅和繼昌隆絲偈幾個問題之我見，南海政協文史資料研究委員會編，南海文史資料，第十輯，1987 年.

曹振中，南海紡織工業史概況，南海政協文史資料研究委員會編，南海文史資料，第十輯，1987 年.

識燕舊，陳启沅軼事三則，南海政協文史資料研究委員會編，南海文史資料，第十輯，1987 年.

王麗娃，近代佛山地區的機器繅絲業對女性觀念的冲擊 佛山檔案與方志，南海市地方志編纂委員會編，南海縣志 北京：中華書局，2000 年. http://www.fsarc.gov.cn/fznj/dqyj/ 201311/t20131112_4462838.html.

陳德華，繼昌隆媒絲廠值得探討的幾個問題，蘇州大學學報，哲學社會版，2000 年，第一期.

陳澹浦，十國機器繅絲機生產鼻祖？佛山日報，2003 年 7 月 12 日.

陳真，姚洛合編，民族資本合創辦和經營的工業，中國近代工業史資料，第一輯，北京，1957 年.

潘衍桐，蠶桑譜序，廣東省南海市南海政協文史資料研究委員會編，蠶桑譜專輯，1994 年.

楊育峰，中國第一代民族工業家陳启沅，中國绿色畫報，2004年，10期.

陳力，八旗文狀元—崇綺，北方文物，2011年 第1期

郭琪，蒙古狀元崇綺的跌宕人㲕，北方文物，2011年第一期.

黃启臣，明清珠江三角洲桑基魚塘發展之緣由，中國生物學史和農學史學术討論會論文.

張志建，南海早期的民族工業—繼昌隆繅絲廠，歷史教學，1986年，第一期.

張茂元，近代珠三角繅絲業技朮變革祖與社會變遷；互枸視角，社會學研究，2007年，第一期.

孫健，中國第一家民族資本近代工業的出現，學術衍究．1979年，第三期.

黎世銘，劉義基編，廣州工商經濟史料，第二輯，廣州文史資料第三十九輯.

Television Series

"Coastal Border Region and Market/International Trade" (海彊與互市), General History of China, Episode 82, CCTV6.

"The Opium War" (鴉片戰爭), General History of China, Episode 96, CCTV6.

"Taiping Rebellion" (太平天國), General History of China. Episode 97, CCTV6.

Appendix 3: Pictures of Chen Family and the House in Xiguan

Figure A.1. Chen Puxuan (3rd son of Chen Qiyuan) and family. Chen Puxuan sitting in the middle, four sons standing from left to right Puseng (蒲生, fourth son), Lianzhong (廉仲, second son), Lianbo (廉伯, oldest son) and Shaoxuan (少軒, third son)

Figure A.2. Chen Ruzhi (9th son of Chen Qiyuan) and his family, in Hong Kong in 1958.
Row 2: Chen Zuohao (作浩, third son) and his wife (L2 and L1); Chen Shaoru (少孺, first son) and his wife (L4 and L3); Chen Ruzhi (陳孺直), and his wife (R5 and L5); Chen Youzhi (幼直, second son) and his wife (R4 and R3); Chen Zuohan (作瀚, fourth son) and his wife (R1 and R2)
Row 3: Chen Xingquan (杏泉, fourth daughter, L1;) Chen Zuocheng (作澄, seventh son) and his wife (L4 and R4) Chen Yongjian (永堅, fifth daughter) and her husband (R3 and R2)

Figure 3: Garden of the Xiquan house where Puxuan and family lived

Figure 4: Garden of the Xiquan house

Figure A.5. Xiquan house from the outside

Figure A.6. Interior of the Xiquan house

Index and Glossary of Terms

Ah Fu 阿福, 93, 107, 134
Ah Liang 阿良, 93, 107, 150
Anhui 安徽, 49
Annam 安南, vii, viii, x, xi, 16, 51–56, 65, 96, 99, 107, 110, 143, 146, 148, 150, 201n33, 202n1, 206n6, 223–225
Antimony 銻, x, 169, 170

Baiyufang 百豫坊, 147–149, 215n2, 241
Beijiang, North River 北江, 34, 170
Beijing (Peking) Covenant 北京盟約, 54
Bicycle Silk-Reeling Machine 脚踏繅絲機, xi, 17, 135, 137–140, 145, 178–179, 186, 190, 214n40, 225
Bien Hoa 邊和市, 62
Black gambiered silk, black Jiao Chou 黑膠綢, 76–77
British East India Company 英國東印度公司, 46
Buluoja 不落家, 182

Cambodia 柬埔寨, 61, 63, 75, 224–225
Can Sang Pu (On Sericulture) 蠶桑譜, 37, 101, 138, 157–159, 174, 224
Canton Street 廣州街, 79, 81
Cash Crops 經濟作物, 150, 188, 189
Catty 斤, 38, 150
Chambon System 尚邦系統, 100, 104–106, 136, 204, 208
Changzan Sizhuang 昌棧絲莊, 112, 145
Chen Danpu 陳淡浦, 99, 101–102, 116, 179, 206n8, 207n12, 219n4
Chen Guangxian 陳光先, 33–34
Chen Hai 陳海, 50
Chen Jijian 陳景建, 155
Chen Jinqiong 陳錦筇, 140
Chen Jinyun 陳錦贇, 224
Chen Jinzan 陳錦簪, 224
Chen Lianchuan 陳濂川, 99
Chen Liantai Company 陳聯泰號, 99

247

Chen Lianzhong 陳廉仲, 166, 239
Chen Puxuan 陳蒲軒, 112, 137, 139–140, 156, 175, 194, 224–225, 239, 241
Chen Qiting Ancestral Hall 陳綺亭公祠, 1–4, 146–147, 149, 193
Chen Qiyuan 陳啟沅, vii, ix–xi, xiii, xv, 1–2, 4–7, 9, 17, 19, 22, 29, 33–34, 42, 50–52, 62, 70, 73–74, 76, 78–79, 81–82, 85, 88, 99, 101–102, 107, 111–112, 116, 123, 127, 130, 137–138, 140, 143–144, 146–149, 150, 153, 155–156, 159, 161, 163–169, 171–172, 174–177, 179, 181, 185–186, 189–190, 193, 198n14, , 205n39, 211n7, 213n33, 223, 225–226, 239–240
Chen Qiyuan Memorial Hall 陳啟沅紀念館, xiii, 2, 34, 38, 102, 105, 107, 137, 146, 149, 150, 153, 168, 172, 193
Chen Qiyuan's Family Tree (The Pedigree of the Chen's Clan) 陳啟沅族譜世系表, 34
Chen Qiyuan's Suan Xue (Chen Qiyuan's Mathematics Book) 陳啟沅算學, 161–162, 225
Chen Ruzhi 陳孺直, vii, xiii, 225, 240
Chen Taochuan 陳桃川, 99
Chen Zhiqu 陳植榘, 123
Chen Zhishu 陳植恕, 123
Chenji Watches and Clocks Repair Expert 陳記精修鐘表, 70
Child Examination 童試, 40–41, 52, 156, 172, 198n13
China Merchants' Steam Navi-gation Company Ltd. 中國招商局輪船有限公司, 130
Cholon, Tai-Ngon 堤岸, xiii, 53, 56, 58–59, 61–66, 70, 72, 74–77, 79, 81, 84, 91–93, 202n7, 223
Chong Qi 崇綺, 166, 173–174, 218n31, 291n40, 291n41
Chongzheng Charity Hall 崇正善堂, 155–156
Cihai 辭海, ix, 34, 197n3
Cochinchina 南圻, 60–63, 75, 224, 225
Confucius 孔子, 37, 39, 60, 115

County magistrate 知縣, 40, 123, 127, 131, 153, 166

Dagang 大崗, 123

Daoguang (Emperor) 道光(皇帝), 47

Denier measure 旦尼爾測量, 104, 190

Diànshì 殿試, 40,

Dongguan 東莞, 21, 35, 119, 111, 188, 192

Dongjiang (East River) 東江, 34

Eight-legged essay 八股文, 39

Erlonghou Garden Road 二龍喉花園馬路, 134

Ever-Victorious Army 常勝軍, 49

Ewo Silk Filature 怡和絲廠, 17–18, 96–97, 107, 110, 206n2

Feng 馮, 33

Filial Piety Classic 孝經, 41

Fire beacon towers 烽火臺, 45

Foshan 佛山, 35, 50, 98, 120, 186, 192

French Indochina or Indo- chinese Union 法屬印度支那, 75, 225

Fuhelong 復和隆, 134, 135

Fujian 福建, 33

God Worshipping Society 拜上帝會, 49

Gong Shuban 公輸班, 173

Gongshi (Tribute Scholar) 貢士, 40

Guande Temple 關帝廟, 123

Guangdong Province 廣東省, vii, x, 11, 17–18, 26, 28, 33, 54, 55, 60, 77, 83, 95–97, 122–123, 127, 132, 150, 158, 160, 169, 171, 173–175, 179–181, 183–184, 217n23, 218n35

Guanglangshu (Arenga pinna- ta, Sugar Palm Tree) 桄榔樹, 5, 6

Guangzhou 廣州, 1, 15–17, 21, 23, 26, 29, 46–47, 50, 77, 85, 91, 97–99, 112, 120–121, 127–128, 133, 145–146, 148, 155–156, 175, 179–180, 186, 189, 192

Guanshan 官山, 111, 126

Guanshan River 官山河, 125, 152

Guanshanxu 官山墟, 125, 150, 151, 155

Guanyunzhang 關雲長, 125

Guizhou 貴州, 26

249

Guo 郭, 33

Hanlin Academy 翰林院, 40
He Gui 何桂, 135
He Lianwang 何連旺, 135, 213n33
Heaven and Earth Society 天地會, 121, 123
Hechang 和昌, 134, 140, 213n33, 224
Hexi Corridor 河西走廊, 11
Hong Xiuquan 洪秀全, 49
Huai Army 淮軍, 49
Huālíng dào xián 花翎道銜, 171, 173
Hue 順化, 59
Huìshì 會試, 40
Huizhou 惠州, 208
Hunan 湖南, 49
Huzhou 湖州, 11, 20

I Ching, The Book of Changes 易經, 147
Imperial Examination 科舉, 39–41, 44, 50, 166, 198n12, 199n15, 218n35

Jiancun 簡村, vii, xi, 1, 2, 16, 33–34, 44, 50, 53, 72, 80, 82, 94, 97–99, 102–103, 116, 125–126, 134–135, 138, 140, 143, 148, 150–152, 175, 177, 187, 189–190, 193, 223–224
Jiangmen 江門, 192
Jiangsu 江蘇, 11, 20, 29
Jiaqing (Emperor) 嘉慶(皇帝), 49
Jichanglong 繼昌隆, xi, 16, 17, Chapter 4, 119, 121–123, 125, 134–135, 137, 139, 143–144, 154, 177, 179, 181–182, 187, 224–225, 207n13, 208n20
Jingluntang 錦綸堂, 120–124, 128
Jinshi, "Advanced Scholars" 進士, 40, 218n35
Jintian 金田, 49
Jishui 吉水, 151–152
Jishui Antrum 吉水竇, 152–153
Joy of Farming 樂耕堂, 2, 7, 37–38, 51, 52, 114, 198n10
Junhechang Sauce Garden 均和昌醬園, 74, 78
Junhezhan Grocery Store 均和棧雜貨店, 65, 69, 202n10
Juren, "Recommended Man" 舉人, 40, 115, 123–124, 127, 210n37

Keqin Yixue 克勤義學, 151

Lake Tai 太湖, 20
Lang Son 諒山, 59
Laos 寮國, 75, 225
Lecong 樂從, 179
Lemire, Charles 勒米爾·查理 (法國人), 62
Li Hongzhang 李鴻章, 49, 131
Li Lou 離婁, 173
Lihousheng 利厚生, 140, 144
Likin 釐金, 24, 28–30, 127, 197n24, 197n26
Lin Zexu 林則徐, 47
Lizhen Silk Filature 利貞絲廠, 139
Longreng 龍仍, 150
Longxi County 龍溪鎮, 33
Lu Jiu 盧九, 133–135, 214n36
Lunyu, Analects of Confucius 論語, 41

Macau (Macao) 澳門, x, xi, 42, 45, 55–56, 97, 132–135, 139, 140, 143–144, 178, 192, 213n33, 224
Maritime Customs Office 海關總稅務司, 47
Mazu 媽祖, 65
Mencius 孟子, 37, 39, 136, 214n39

Microscript 微書, 165–166, 173, 218n30, 218n33, 218n34
Mok 莫, 33
Mu (Chinese) (華) 畝, 36
Mui-tsai 妹仔, 82
Mulberry and Silkworm Garden 蠶桑園, 2, 5, 6

Nanhai 南海, vii–ix, xi, 1, 2, 16–18, 21, 29–30, 33–37, 51, 99, 116, 119–121, 123, 127–132, 135, 139, 140, 145, 158, 165, 176–177, 179, 180, 186–188, 196n8, 223–224
Nanjing Treaty 南京條約, 47, 50
Nguyen Dynasty 阮氏王朝, 91

Opium 鴉片, 46–47, 63
 First Opium War 第一次鴉片戰爭, 48, 54, 120–121, 223
 Second Opium War 第二次鴉片戰爭, 111, 112, 130, 223–224

Pan Yantong 潘衍桐, 158
Panyu 番禺, 120, 186

Pebrine silkworm disease 蠶微粒子病, 14, 84, 195n4
Pendulum clock 擺鐘, 42–43, 66–68, 199n16
Picul 擔, 12–13, 22, 25, 28–29, 124, 145, 163, 178
Polaris 北極星, 57
Prajnaparamita Hrdaya Sutra 般若波羅密多心經, 166
Puji, Universal Charity Hall 普濟善堂, 155

Qianlong (Emperor) 乾隆(皇帝), 65
Qibiao 啟標, 36, 52, 53
Qing Army 清軍, 49, 50, 59
Qing Dynasty 清朝, 20, 36, 44–45, 54, 120, 150, 155, 159, 164, 186, 198n12, 200n23, 218n29
Qing government 清政府, 28, 39, 46–48, 49, 59, 83, 86, 95, 130, 133–134, 199n19
Qishu 啟樞, 36, 51–53, 56, 58, 63, 65–66, 69, 78, 90, 134, 140, 146, 201n33, 201n34, 201n35, 205n37, 223
Qiushuǐ xuan chidu 秋水軒尺牘, 41, 198n12

Records of the Three Kingdoms 三國志, 166

Saigon 西貢, 59, 61–63, 66, 69, 72, 74–75, 84, 91–93, 202n7, 223
San Ho Hui, Triple Union Society 三合會, 50
Sanshui 三水, 21, 127, 132, 188
Self-Strengthening Movement 自強運動, 24, 95, 130, 140, 213n26, 240
Sericin 絲膠, 9–10, 100, 136
Sericulture 養蠶業, ix, 9, 11–12, 14, 16, 20–21, 25, 36–37, 83, 96, 139, 150, 157, 160, 180, 188, 192, 210n1, 217n22, 220n11, 224
Shang dynasty 商朝, 11, 37
Shanghai, 15–20, 22, 23, 26, 28–29, 49, 96, 107, 112, 130, 183, 192, 196n10, 206n2
Shaoquan 韶關, x, 169, 170, 225
Shenbao 申報, 130
Shengqixiang Rice Store 盛其祥谷米行, 78
Shengyuan 生員 or "Cultivated Talent" 秀才, 40
Shenzhen 深圳, 192

Shisanhang 十三行, 99
Shiwan 石灣, 179
Shoushitang 壽世堂, 151
Shun (Emperor) 舜(帝), 37
Shunde 順德, 17–19, 21, 26, 29–30, 35, 97–98, 111, 116, 119, 121, 127, 132, 145, 158, 178–181, 184, 188, 196n9, 196n12, 197n20, 206n3, 219n7, 220n8
Si-shu 私塾, 2, 7, 37–38, 51–52, 114, 151, 156, 201n31, 223
Sichanglun 世昌綸, 141, 144, 215n46
Sifu Temple 師傅廟, 123
Siheyuan 四合院, 2, 195n3
Silk Weavers' Riot 絲織工的暴動, xi, 17, Chatter 5, 178, 186
Sin 冼, 33
Sishu Wujing, Four Books and Five Classics 四書五經, 41, 198n13
Sizhuang 絲莊, 112, 145, 209n31
Song Dynasty 宋朝, 11, 44
Survey 測量, 164, 169–171, 218n37, 225
Suzhou 蘇州, 20
Suzhou-Jiaxing 蘇州-嘉興, 20

Taels 兩, 51, 71, 85, 99, 108, 110, 128, 134, 140, 145, 153–154, 206n6
Taiping Heavenly Kingdom 太平天國, 49
Taiping Rebellion 太平天國叛亂, 49–50, 95, 121, 201n28
Taishan 台山, 90
Tao Mo 陶模, 169, 171, 175, 218n35
Tarim Basin 塔里木盆地, 11
Tavelle System 塔維爾系統, 136, 204n33
Tay Son dynasty 西山(阮)朝, 75
The Nine Chapters on the Mathematical Art 九章算術, 163
The Origin of Liqi 理氣溯源, 164
The Unique Fellow of Nanhai 南海畸人, 165
Theodolite 經緯儀, 170
Thousand Character Classic 千字文, 41
Three Character Classic 三字經, 41
Tibetan Red Flower 西藏紅花, 175

253

Tin Hau Temple 天后廟, or Apocheon Temple 阿婆廟, 64
Tokyo Zhuang 東京莊, 78
Tongzhi(Emperor) 同治皇帝, 20, 166, 218n35

Understanding the Theories of I-Ching 周易理數會通, 164

Vietnam 越南, vii, 51, 58–62, 74–77, 80–83, 85, 89, 91–92, 93, 95, 150, 203n19, 203n21, 223–224

Wang Zhiwen 王芝文, 166
Warington Smyth, Herbert 瓦靈頓·史米斯·赫爾伯特, 57
Western Han Dynasty 西漢, 11, 78
Wu Feng 吳封, 159
Wuti (Emperor) (漢)武帝, 59
Wuxi 無錫, 20, 29, 192
Wuxi-Changzhou 無錫-常州, 20

Xiang Army 湘軍, 49
Xiāngshì 鄉試, 40
Xiǎo Táng Zhè Gû Gǎng, "The Little Pond on Partridge Hill" 小塘鷓鴣崗, 176
Xie Yuqin 謝玉琴, 166
Xijiang, West River 西江, 34
Xindoulan Sheng Jie 新豆欄上街, 99
Xingtou 杏頭, 150–152
Xiqiao 西樵, vii, 1, 2, 16, 26, 33, 36–37, 93–94, 99, 111, 120, 126, 129, 152, 177, 223
Xu Feng 許鋒, ix–x, 213n33
Xu Gengbi 徐賡陛, 127–129, 131
Xu Jiacun 許葭村, 198n12
Xuetang 學堂, 115–116, 123–129, 131, 211n8

Yi Yin 伊尹, 37
Yichangyin Silk Store 怡昌蔭號紗綢, 78
Yifeng Pawnshop 怡豐餉當, 81
Yongshenghao 永生號, 150,
Yuchang 裕昌, 78
Yuhouchang 裕厚昌, 123–125, 127

Zeng Guofan 曾國藩, 49
Zhang 丈, 103, 115
Zhaoqing 肇慶, 192

Zhejiang 浙江, 11, 20, 26, 29, 218n35
Zheng He 鄭和, 45
Zhongshan 中山, 192
Zhu Di (Emperor) 朱棣(皇帝), 45
Zhu Yuanzhang (Emperor) 朱元漳(皇帝), 33
Zhuangyuan 狀元, 166
Zhuhai 珠海, 192
Zhujiang, Pearl River 珠江, 34
Zhuzi baijia, Various Sages and Hundred Schools of Thought 諸子百家, 41
Zishunu 自梳女, 182–183
Zongli Yamen 總理衙門, 169

www.ingramcontent.com/pod-product-compliance
Lightning Source LLC
Chambersburg PA
CBHW020633220526
45464CB00001B/131